2012

2012

Office Interiors

Edition 2007

Author: Pilar Chueca
Editor: Carles Broto
Editorial coordinator: Jacobo Krauel
Graphic design & production: Dimitris Kottas
Text: contributed by the architects, edited and translated
by William George and Jay Noden

© Carles Broto i Comerma
Jonqueres, 10, 1-5
08003 Barcelona, Spain
Tel.: +34 93 301 21 99
Fax: +34 93 301 00 21
E-mail: info@linksbooks.net
www. linksbooks.net

Office Interiors

LINKS

Index

Introduction

The work environment, as a space for professional and interpersonal exchange, has undergone dramatic changes in recent years. The continuing swift pace of developments in communication technology, with a new, more timeless, ubiquitous and portable handling of information, has greatly contributed to these changes. Gone are the bulky file cabinets and expansive tables of yesteryear, with work surfaces having been reduced to the size of a computer. Tele-work and videoconferencing are further indications of this omnipresence.

At the same time, however, is an ever-increasing trend towards sustainability in architecture, as evidenced by energy-saving measures, alternative energy sources and the use of new materials.

These, and a host of additional concerns particular to office design, greet the architect and interior designers when drawing up the plans for a new workspace. The company's corporate identity, for example, must be somehow translated into the volumes of the interior spaces, as well as of the building as a whole. The modern office also requires versatility and dynamism – it must be flexible enough to quickly adapt to a range of uses. It must be aesthetically pleasing, and should encourage interpersonal communication amongst employees, while significantly lessening outdated hierarchical barriers. Such is the case in the program designed by Carlos Manzano, with its city-like structure, complete with avenues, a central square and a port. Klein Dytham's design has opted for horseshoe shaped workstations which can accommodate up to 85 people a day, thereby eliminating private offices.

In short, this is a concise, yet wide-ranging, volume, bringing together examples of renovated spaces as well as entirely new ground plans – proposals which comprise an invaluable source of inspiration and a concentrated study of the challenges involved in creating new workspaces.

Neil M. Denari Architects Inc.

Endeavor

Beverly Hills, California, USA

Photographs:
Benny Chan / Fotoworks

Located within a 1961 Charles Luckman building in downtown Beverly Hills, this interiors project consists of 5860 sqm (63 000 sqft) of offices for nearly 200 people and an 80 seat screening room. Endeavor is the third largest talent agency in the world and the company represents a wide range of writers, directors, and actors including Martin Scorsese and Paul Thomas Anderson. Their primary competition, CAA, falls on the conservative side of the spectrum in the entertainment industry, while Endeavor has a younger and more progressive image, which the firm wanted to reflect in the design of their new space.

The layout is based on the dimensions of the existing building and the necessary visual and acoustical connection between the agent and his/her assistant. The agents have window offices along the perimeter with their assistants situated within the adjacent open office space. The circulation has to provide access to all offices between the agent and their assistant. The shared workstations are situated so that each assistant looks diagonally into the agent's office. A sectional raise toward the perimeter and a band of clerestory glass in the open office space creates excellent natural lighting conditions for the assistant's area. The two-story office is divided into four distinct zones (two per floor). Given the repetitious nature of the office layout, a wayfinding or coding system became a necessary feature. Each of the four zones is given a general color range (Magenta, Cyan, Orange and Green) to orient the agents and their visitors. Walls perpendicular to the length of the building are saturated with these colors, including special wallpaper graphics on the secondary cores. These images were developed in collaboration with 2×4, a New York based graphic design company.

The screening room consists not only of a high performance space for viewing films, but also a large pre function lobby area, a kitchen/bar, and a major façade to the street. The intention was to make what is essentially a private space become more public. This serves two purposes: One is to create as much spatial depth as possible in the entry sequence so as to break down the flatness of the "storefront" conditions surrounding it. The other is to create a public identity for Endeavor in a way that the offices cannot. The folded aluminum panel façade and the smooth, white undulating ceiling and wall surfaces that form the first 10 ft of the space allow passersby to catch fragments of the floor and ceiling surfaces inside. The exterior wall of the screening room is wrapped with wallpaper designed by 2×4, while the interior is a deeply saturated red world consisting of different materials and textures of paint, carpet, and fabric.

Architects:
Neil M. Denari Architects Inc.
Project team:
Neil Denari & Duks Koschitz
with Stefano Paiocchi,
Jae Shin, Matt Trimble,
Steven Epley, Betty Kassis
Graphics: Brennan Buck
Interior Architects:
Bruce Campbell, David Leckie
Graphic Design:
2×4 NY, Michael Rock,
Glen Cummings
Structural engineer:
Matti J Prabhu & Associates
Inc: Matti J Prabhu
Mechanical and electrical engineer:
Syska Hennessy Group;
Hisham Barakat
Lighting Design:
Lighting Design Alliance;
Archit Jain
Project Manager:
Anthony Mason Associates;
Anthony Mason,
Kryste Kurlander
Acoustical Consultant:
M. Newson & Associates;
Martin Newson, Michael
Brown, Derreck Hendrix
AV Consultant:
Rail Productions;
Isaac Levenbrown
Client:
Endeavor

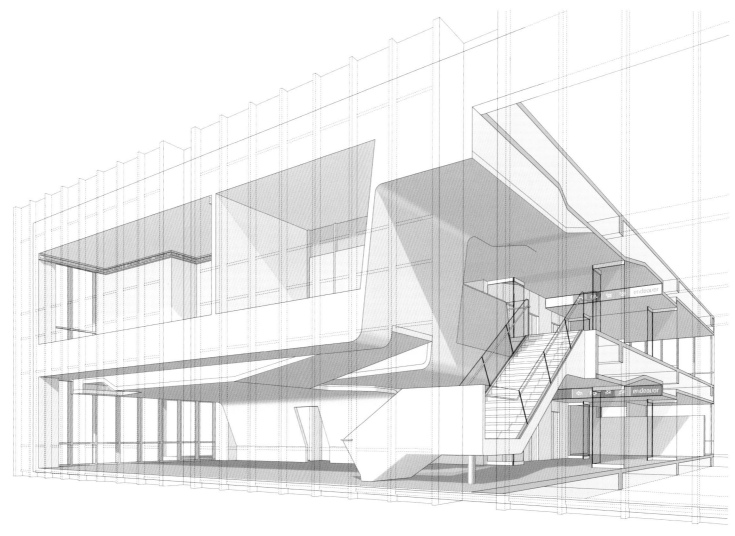

Given the straight forward planning dictated by the build-ing, the more expressive aspects of the project can be found in ceiling / wall deformations surrounding the main lobby and conference room areas, and in the core ele-ments that float within the field.

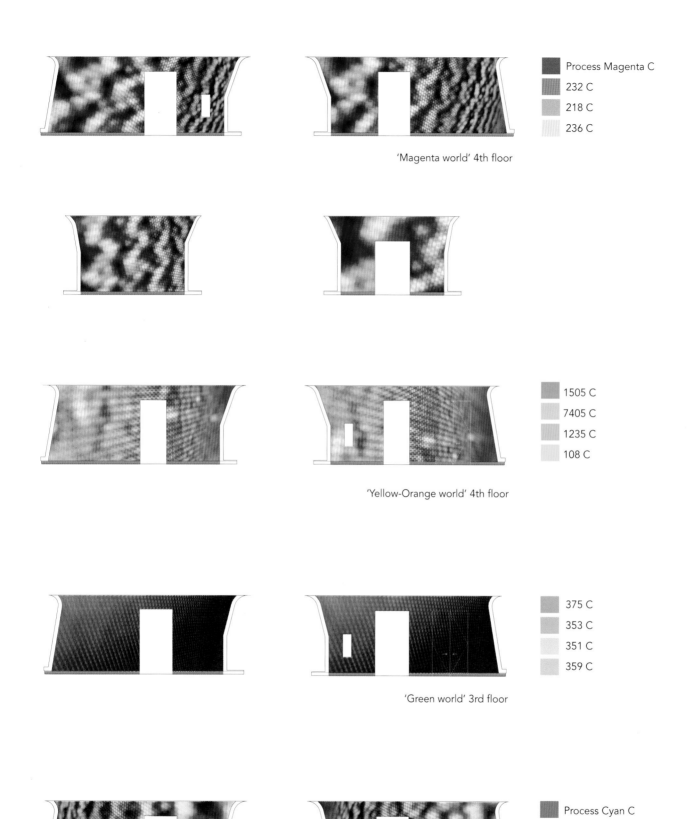

Process Magenta C
232 C
218 C
236 C

'Magenta world' 4th floor

1505 C
7405 C
1235 C
108 C

'Yellow-Orange world' 4th floor

375 C
353 C
351 C
359 C

'Green world' 3rd floor

Process Cyan C
2995 C
305 C
2975 C

'Blue world' 3rd floor

Neil M. Denari Architects Inc.   **13**

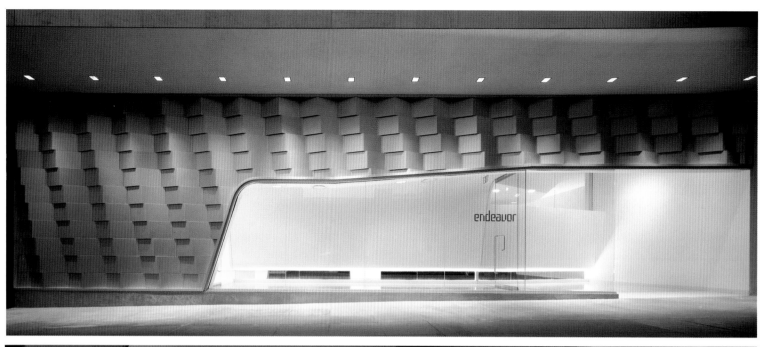

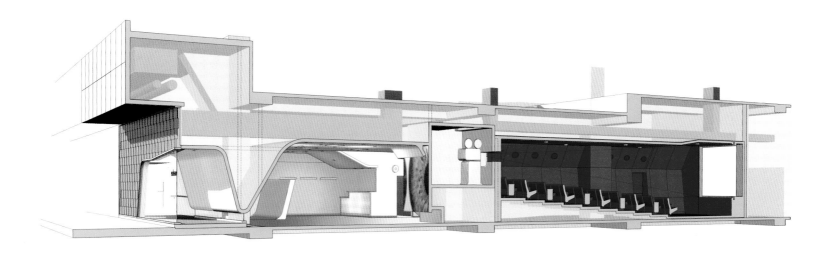

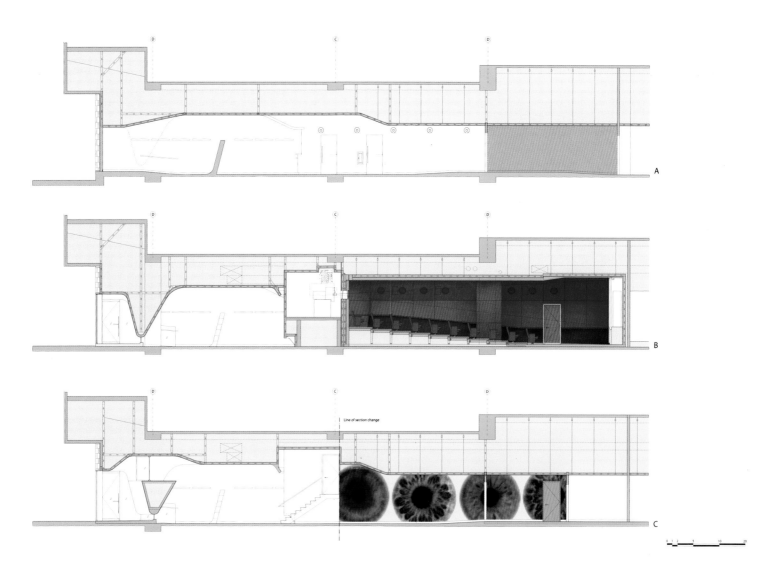

A

B

C

Line of section change

The exterior wall of the screening room is wrapped with wallpaper designed by 2×4. The interior is a deeply saturated red world consisting of different materials and textures of paint, carpet, and fabric.

Stefano Marinelli, Lucio Massignan + Archingegno

Adotta

Vicenza, Italy

Photographs:
Maurizio Marcato

Adotta is a company that processes and builds glazed walls. In their new premises, a renovated 1960's warehouse, the light source becomes architecture. The shell is a large oblong structure with a vaulted roof, a 1200 sqm (12900 sqft) footprint and some 1000 sqm (10760 sqft) of offices and exhibition spaces on three levels. Starting from a programmed design, the new inner walls of the workstations were made of glass: behind them, a luminous wall closing the northern end of the building provides a background. Transparency and reflections on the glazed surfaces and the polished concrete floor create a suggestive, homogeneous atmosphere. Every detail contributes to balance the plastic and evocative potential of the light source.

From the main ground floor entrance, a luminous trail cut through the ceiling penetrates every space and conducts the visitor towards the great three-floor stairway. The interior looks like a department store or a museum, centered on the long straight stairway, which consists of several flights leading to the highest level. Light is strategically set at the background wall's corners, to interrupt the room's unity, introducing a new spatial logic by means of a plastic relief and a sequence of 160 fluorescent tubes. The staircase, with a black PVC floor, and the constant luminous trail, enliven the vertical or horizontal surfaces. Lines are clear and defined, with gaps and corners that multiply the view points. Under the vaulted roof of the whole building, three air-light ducts distribute the air-conditioning; made of white polyester and containing a double row of fluorescent lamps, these ducts become subtle and effective diffuser lamps.

Architecture:
Stefano Marinelli, Lucio
Massignan with Archingegno
Light installation:
Carlo Ferrari + Alberto
Pontiroli
www.archingegno.info
Client:
Adotta del gruppo Trevisan
Cometal, viale del Lavoro 12,
Vicenza, Italy
Surface area:
1200 sqm (12900 sqft)
Cronology:
2003-2004

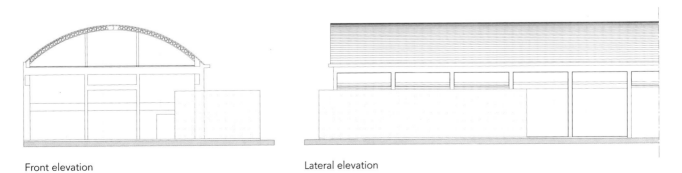

Front elevation

Lateral elevation

Stefano Marinelli, Lucio Massignan + Archingegno

1. Primary entrance
2. Distributive corridor
3. Stair to upper level
4. Multimedia room
5. Meeting room
6. Communication office
7. Offices
8. Storages
9. Bathrooms
10. Empty space
11. Showroom

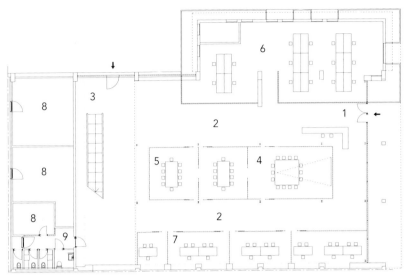

Ground floor plan

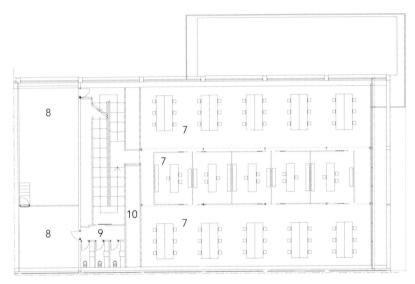

First floor plan

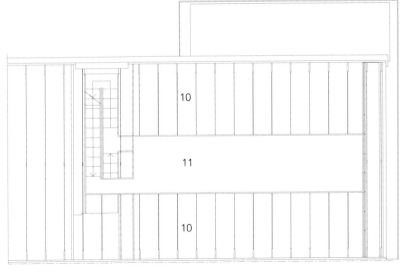

Second floor plan

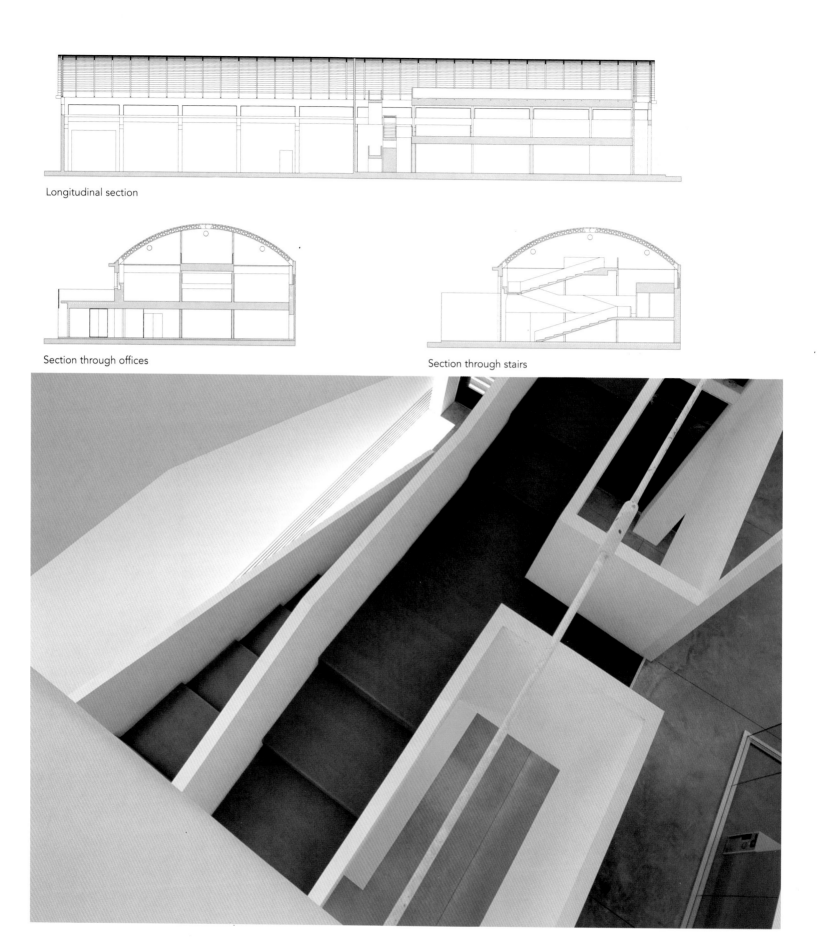

Longitudinal section

Section through offices

Section through stairs

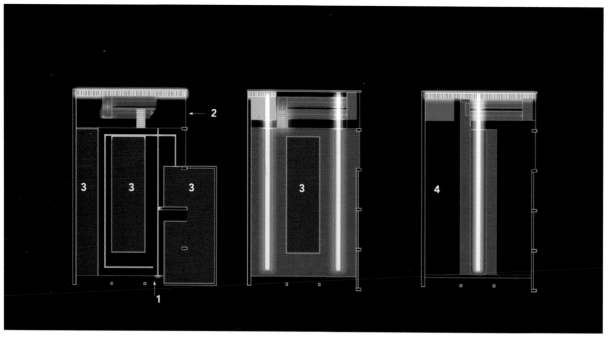

Ground floor   First floor   Second floor

 Fuorescent light
Fuorescent continuous light T16
Light-air volume

1. Primary entrance
2. Secondry entrance
3. Independent work spaces
4. Empty space on first level

The first floor is a wide open space, lit by the translucent air-light ducts. The meeting rooms, in the center, occupy the glazed cubicles underneath the mezzanine; there are workstations at the sides and, suspended in the middle of the stairway, is a grey cube that contains the toilet facilities. The neutral image allows the spaces and their different shades of light to speak for themselves.

The luminous trail consists of a sequence of 160 plain fluorescent lamps with a 40 cm interval. Protected by glass, the trail of light set in the floor can be walked on. The project underlines the possibility of shaping space out of light. As stated by the artist James Turrell: "Space is shaped by light's setting and position; its creation is related to man." In this project, light becomes a building material.

Christian Pottgiesser

Forest through the table

Paris, France

Photographs:
Luc Boegly

The project accommodates the headquarters of two companies in Paris - PONS and HUOT - with a total of fifteen executives between the two. Consequently, the designers have provided the unit with seven private offices for each of the managers and a large workroom for the remaining eight members of the staff. In addition there is a meeting-room (divisible), a shared recreational room, a kitchen, rest rooms, and, at the special request of the client, luxuriant vegetation throughout the main space.

The starting point was a derelict industrial hall built in the late 19th century with a steel framework typical of the period, and a glass roof that was on the verge of collapse. Rumor has it that it was designed by none other than Gustave Eiffel.

To start with, the hall was completely restored. A new glass roof was fitted (Mannesman/KDI "Fineline", Pilkington "Activ Suncool", self-cleaning), and all the main features of the building was put back into their original state.

Finally, the project itself consists of inserting into the existing shell a wooden unit made of solid oak, 1.7 m high, 22 m long and 14 m wide (0.57 × 7.34 × 4.67 ft). The entire program is embodied therein. Each individual workplace is incised into the wooden upper surface and covered by a "telephone'-dome in Plexiglas. The four lateral surfaces contain filing systems, cloakrooms and the kitchen. Completely embedded in the body are the meeting room, the recreational room and the restrooms. The remaining space is taken up by technical transmission systems (computer, electricity, air condition, heating and water) and also by 18.3 cubic meters (646 cubic feet) of soil, the bed for eight Ficus Panda trees.

Entrance hall and reception areas were omitted, as visitors are guided by a peripheral path-system that leads to all the pertinent rooms. The individual offices are situated on the two mezzanine galleries.

Architect:
Christian Pottgiesser
Architecturespossibles
Team:
Christian Pottgiesser, architect
Pascale Pottgiesser, artist
Florian Hertweck, assistant
Matthieu Lott, assistant
Total floor area:
540 sqm (5810 sqft)
180 sqm (1936 sqft) mezzanine

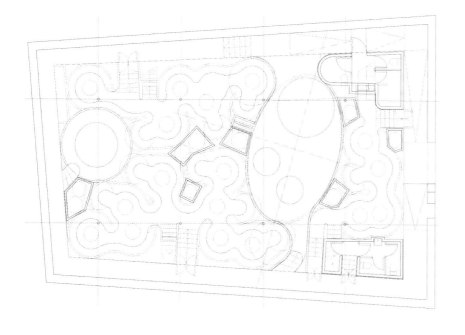

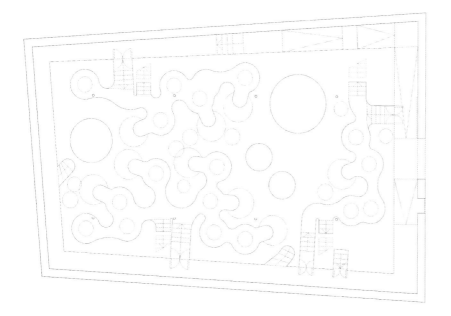

The starting point was a derelict industrial hall built in the late 19th century with a steel framework typical of the period, and a glass roof that was on the verge of collapse. Rumor has it that it was designed by none other than Gustave Eiffel.

The hall was completely restored. A new glass roof was fitted (Mannesman/KDI "Fineline", Pilkington "Activ Suncool", self-cleaning).

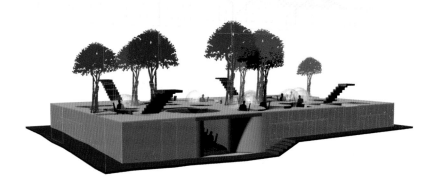

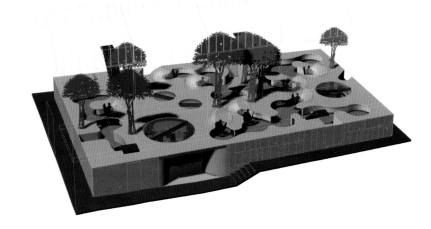

Once the main features of the building had been returned to their original state, a wooden unit made of solid oak, 1.7 m high, 22 m long and 14 m wide, was inserted into the existing shell, to contain the entire program. Each individual workplace is incised into the wooden upper surface and covered by a "telephone'-dome in Plexiglas.

The completed project provides seven private offices for the seven managers and a large workroom for the remaining eight members of the staff. In addition there is a meeting-room (divisible), a shared recreational room, the kitchen, and the rest rooms. The client requested luxuriant vegetation throughout the main space. Entrance hall and reception areas were omitted, as visitors follow a peripheral path-system that leads to all the pertinent rooms. The managerial offices are situated on the two mezzanine levels.

Aguirre Newman Arquitectura

Affinity

Sant Cugat del Vallés, Barcelona, Spain

Photographs:
Jordi Miralles

Design and construction management:
Aguirre Newman Arquitectura
Interiors:
Wolf Ollins

The project addresses the new headquarters of a pet-food merchandizing enterprise, located on two floors of a building by the architect Eduardo Gascón. The objective of the new offices has to achieve the well-being and comfort of the employees using domestic accessories, so they would feel at home, a home that is comfortable, contemporary, flexible and practical.

The offices are distributed on two rectangular floors, with the communications and technical systems grouped around a central nucleus. These floors, which already had the basic HVAC installations (air-conditioning, safety lighting, technical floor and double ceiling) have been organized according to one same concept: to do without the offices as such for everybody to work together without visual constraints, facilitating meeting areas of a formal and informal nature, enhancing the exchange of information. A clear zoning has been established, which comprises two main open areas for work and two mixed use areas near the centralized access. Adjacent to the nucleus are the reception desk, the visitors hall and the cafeteria. The only hierarchic concession is the position of the managerial areas, situated around the perimeter, individualized yet open as well. The few enclosed spaces are the meeting rooms, waiting rooms and visitor attention rooms, which are built of lightweight plasterboard, aluminum and glass.

This open plan enables natural light to penetrate every corner and the wide windows incorporate the views of the landscape into the works environment. Decoration of the work zones, with neutral tones and curvy, ergonomically designed furniture, stresses warmth. These areas are only differentiated from the rest by the flooring material, a surface of small wooden slats similar to industrial parquet.

Thus, the offices have become an interactive, socializing space, enhancing informal encounters, the exchange of information and the generation of ideas.

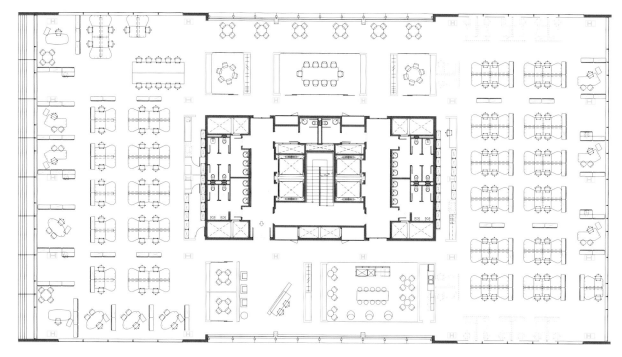

Third floor plan

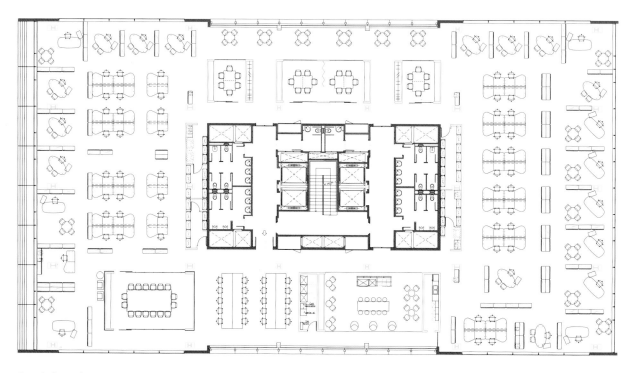

Fourth floor plan

The project addresses the new headquarters of a pet-food merchandizing enterprise, located on two floors of a building by the architect Eduardo Gascón.

For the meeting rooms, the free standing height has been lowered with an acoustic ceiling and plush carpeting, besides roll-up screens that provide the necessary privacy and allow projections to take place with the desirable control of ambient luminosity. One of these rooms is enclosed in a wall of beech wood slats, which distinguishes it from the rest.

A characteristic sign of the installation is a large canvas with colored images of cats and dogs, which clads the centralized technical nucleus and creates an appropriate backdrop for all the zones of the office.

For the sales service, a container-room has been implemented, entirely clad in stainless steel doggy-bowls. Opposite the reception desk a wall has been designed with strips of different colors, which consist in fact of a continuous repetition of the labels of the brand's products.

The main theme of the enterprise, dogfood and catfood, has generated details such as the "teaching wall" in the cafeteria, decorated with exchangeable panels with descriptions of the breeds of these pets, for the employees to become familiar with their characteristics.

Mother

London, UK

Photographs:

Adrian Wilson

Mother is a young but significant British advertising agency whose radical approach to the advertising business and contemporary culture has translated into their work environment. The company boasts a flat organization with no space privileges; everyone working around a single large worktable. As the advertising agency has grown so has the table.

Clive Wilkinson Architects was awarded the project of redesigning Mother's work premises in a three-story warehouse covering 3900 sqm (42000 sqft) in Shoreditch, London. The client elected to use the 2nd floor as their primary workspace due to the existing enhanced 13 ft floor height and a large 1300 sqm (14000 sqft) open area. In order to achieve a strong connection to the loading bay lobby, two floors below, the team of architects proposed to build a new concrete staircase the width of a small road, which cuts through the building and connects the three floors. This 4.65 m (14 ft) wide staircase would turn into the Agency's cast-in-place concrete worktable and circuit the third floor room like a racetrack. At 84 meters (250 feet) long it has become perhaps the world's largest table with a maximum capacity of 200 people. Due to its enormous dimensions it has been broken in sections to aid circulation. The inspiration for the concrete table was the iconic 1920's Giacomo Matte-Trucco roof top race track for Fiat Lingotto in Turin.

On all floors, all surfaces were painted white, with a white epoxy floor, to achieve a neutral art studio space. To mitigate sound in the hard factory space, the architects designed 7-foot long lampshades padded with 3 inches of acoustic foam. The fifty light fixtures were then covered with fifty different patterns of Marimekko fabric, achieving the effect of a large art installation, which is all the more striking in a space where everything else is white. On other floors, customized plastic refrigeration curtains were used to subdivide spaces for different disciplines and subsidiary companies.

The project was expedited in construction and delivered on a tight budget. The reduced density and added meeting spaces have helped the agency to work more smoothly, and voice acoustics in the table area have been effectively controlled through the padded lights.

Architects:
Clive Wilkinson Architects
Project Team:
Clive Wilkinson,
Richard Hammond
Client:
Mother Advertising Ltd
Developer and Landlord:
Simon Silver, Derwent Valley PLC
Project Manager:
Jackson Coles
Executive Architect:
AHMMA (Allford Hall
Monaghan Morris Architects)
MEP Engineers:
Cundall Johnston & Partners LLP
General Contractor:
SAMES plc
Plastic Screens:
Safety Screens
Marimekko Covers:
Marj Abela
Millwork:
Roger Hynam: Wall of doors,
white leather ottomans;
David Hall: Stainless reception
desk and bar
Floor Finish: Polyurethane
paint by Thortex
Date Project Completed:
February 2004
Total surface:
3900 sqm (42000 sqft)

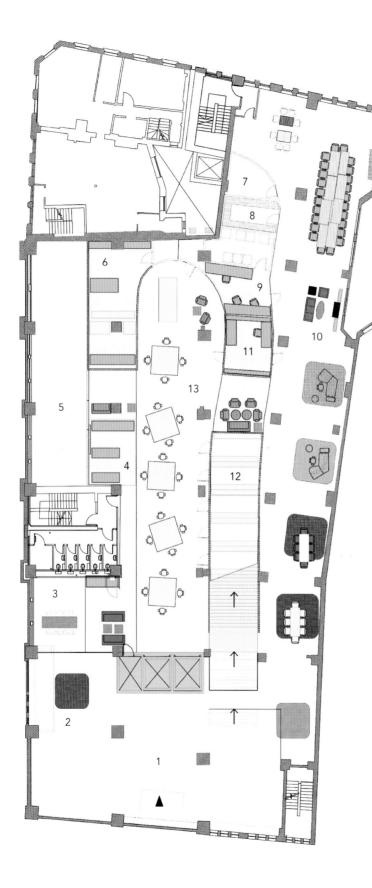

Second floor plan

1. Entry Lobby
2. Cafe
3. Coffee Bar
4. Shipping/Courier Area
5. Play Area
6. Portfolio Storage
7. Storage
8. Office Supplies
9. IT Room
10. "The Living Room"
11. Info Center
12. File Folder Storage
13. Studio

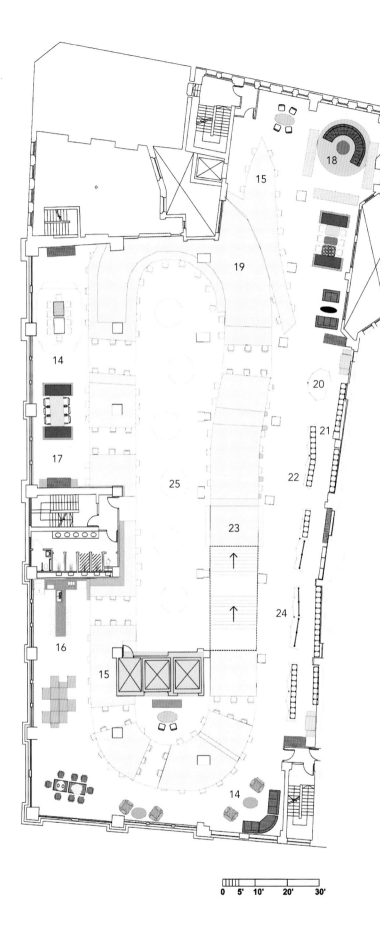

Third floor plan

14. Break-out Spaces
15. Table
16. Coffee Bar
17. Printer/fax
18. "The War Room"
19. Sloping Table
20. Phone Booth
21. Personal Lockers
22. Display Walls
23. Landing
24. Laptop/Mobile Phone Issue
25. Ottomans

0   5'   10'   20'   30'

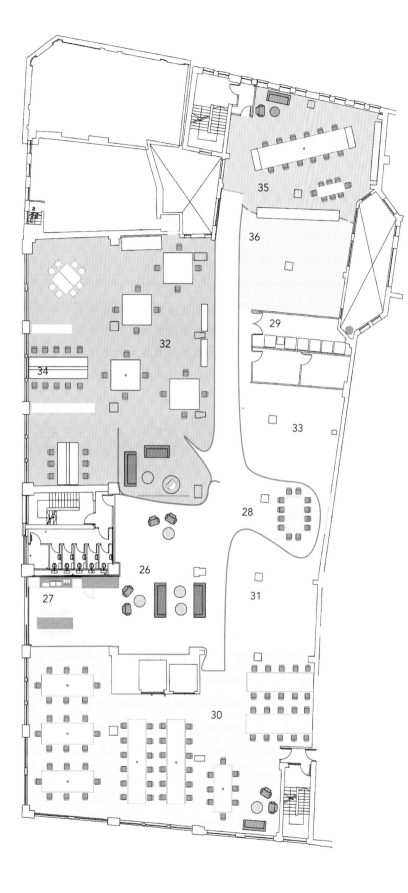

Fourth floor plan

26. Reception
27. Coffee Bar
28. Shared Meeting Space
29. IT Room
30. Subsidiary Company #1
31. Expansion Space #1
32. Subsidiary Company #2
33. Expansion Space #2
34. Freelancer's Table
35. Subsidiary Company #3
36. Expansion Space #3

In order to achieve a strong connection to the loading bay lobby, two floors below, the team of architects proposed to build a new concrete staircase the width of a small road. This 14 ft wide staircase would turn into the Agency's cast-in-place concrete worktable and circuit the 3rd floor room like a racetrack. At 250 feet long it has become perhaps the world's largest table with a maximum capacity of 200 people. The inspiration for the concrete table was the iconic 1920's Giacomo Matte-Trucco roof top race track for Fiat Lingotto in Turin.

On all floors, all surfaces were painted white, with a white epoxy floor, to achieve a neutral art studio space. To mitigate sound in the hard factory space, the architects designed 7-foot long lampshades padded with 3 inches of acoustic foam. The fifty light fixtures were then covered with fifty different patterns of Marimekko fabric, achieving the effect of a large art installation, which is all the more striking in a space where everything else is white.

Teeple Architects and Superkül Inc | Architect

St Joseph Media

Toronto, Canada

Photographs:
Tom Arban

Architects:
Teeple Architects and
Superkül Inc | Architect
Completion:
September 2004
Surface:
3250 sqm (35 000 sqft)

The challenge to the architects in this project was to bring together under one roof nearly 300 employees of twelve different publications, hitherto located in separate offices scattered around Toronto, Canada's largest city. The merger of two companies Multi-Vision Publishing and Key Media resulted in St Joseph Media, the largest privately owned consumer magazine publisher in Canada, responsible for popular, well-established magazines like Toronto Life, Fashion Magazine, Gardening Life and Where Canada. The brief was to bring these satellite companies into one space, make them feel part of the same company while retaining their individuality.

The given space was 3250 sqm (35 000 sqft) comprising two floors in a nineteenth century industrial building which had fallen into disrepair before being converted into the Queen Richmond Centre. Originally a complex of small buildings sharing brick party walls, in a major refurbishment they had been interconnected into a single complex.

The pockets formed by these thick masonry walls were an obvious element to use to create separate homes for each magazine. Floors were misaligned, ceiling heights inconsistent and in addition the windows were mostly on the exterior walls of the original building, so the inner areas were short of light. The architects resolved this by breaking through the floor plate and linking the two floors beneath a new, full-length skylight, creating a long corridor, almost like an internal main street. In this way the individual magazines have kept their own identity but have been united, connected by corridor and skylight. Staff can be focused on their own projects while feeling part of a large, supportive company with all the extra resources and stimulation that it entails, to say nothing of the natural light that floods into their offices.

The reception area is a strategic point in the corridor and large stairways at each end connect the floors, striking visual features in steel and acrylic. This space is wrapped with patterned glass, and felt is used to absorb sound and for magazine logos and signs. These new interventions form a sleek counterpoint to the raw materials of the original warehouse, though respect for the 19th century elements has been shown. The interior brick has been sand blasted, wooden floors sanded and sealed and some of the timber structures retained to give a sense of industrial loft space.

This luminous, striking design, by Teeple Architects in association with Superkul Inc | Architect not only met the client's pragmatic objectives but won Best of Canada Design Award in 2005 from Canadian Interiors magazine as well as a Design Exchange Award. Teeple Architects and Superkül Inc | Architect are known for their exceptional material and spatial quality as illustrated in this particular project.

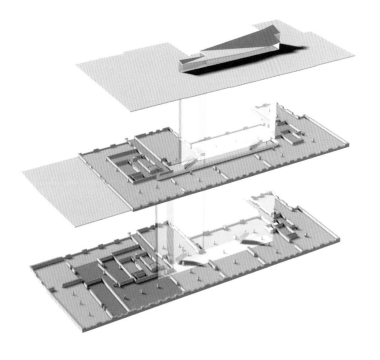

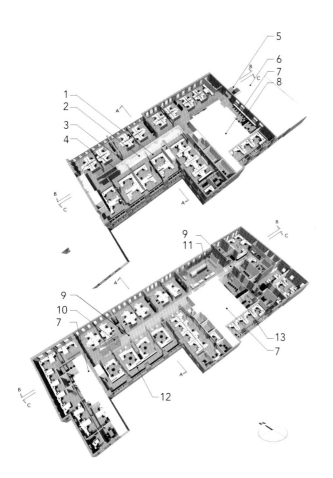

1. Street
2. Opening to below with skylight above
3. Glass enclosure
4. Stair to third floor
5. Stair to third floor and roof deck
6. Future roof deck
7. Building core
8. Staff lounge
9. Street - reference area
10. Stair to fourth floor
11. Reception
12. Typical magazine pod with workstations
13. Boardroom

The reception area is a strategic point in the corridor and large stairways at each end connect the floors, striking visual features in steel and acrylic. This space is wrapped with patterned glass, and felt is used to absorb sound and for magazine logos and signs.

North – south section AA

East – west section BB looking north

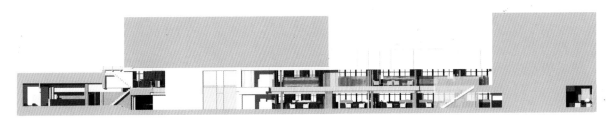

East – west section CC looking south

Pugh + Scarpa

Jigsaw

Los Angeles, California, USA

Photographs:
Marvin Rand

The film editing profession requires small, dark environments free from distraction and light reflection in essence, hermetically sealed boxes. Yet at the same time, a film editing company, if it is to be competitive, must exist in a stimulating, socially interactive workspace, alive to workers and clients alike a place where people will want to be.

This was the challenge laid down for the architects; to transform the interior of a rough 1940's 465 sqm (5000 sqft) bow-truss warehouse into an entirely surprising and inventive space for film editing company, Jigsaw. The location of the warehouse in a featureless, industrial area of West Los Angeles created few basic restrictions, yet the question of how to incorporate box-like rooms inside a large area while simultaneously creating an alive, interior atmosphere became a major challenge.

To answer this question, the architect's first decision was to treat the building's warehouse exterior as a kind of horizon or envelope within which to locate a large interior public area, which would enclose the warehouse's smaller rooms. Incorporating the client's program of offices, library, socializing zones, music rooms and editing rooms, the design uses independent forms as well as interior walls of unique materials, to create an entirely new and unexpected world of public and private space. The dull West Los Angeles neighborhood surrounding the warehouse is at once replaced inside, through a variety of volumes and forms, all kept below ceiling height.

The variety of informal spaces incorporated in the design allows clients and staff to have spaces to relax and to socialize. In addition, the entire entrance zone acts as a café that facilitates informal meetings and client interaction. Social activity is thrown into the limelight. On the opposite side of the café is the reception area, growing out of the linoleum floor material. The reception desk is deliberately moved from the entrance door, encouraging the visitor to absorb the space freely immediately.

The central design elements are the two oblong skewed boxes hovering over a placid reflecting pool. These gently curving structures enclose the editing studios and offices. Facing the lobby, the ends present a luminous textured façade, which are revealed on closer inspection to be panels filled respectively with ping-pong balls and acrylic beads. The interstices created by the volumes undulating over the shimmering plane of water evoke Venetian canals and Richard Serra's torqued ellipses. A discreet circular "fountain" sunk into the pool fills the space with the soothing sound of running water.

The design of Jigsaw attempts to create a series of balanced tensions – between isolation and interaction, movement and static, light and heavy and between light and dark, generating a complex spatial experience, turning an office space into an inspiring playground.

Architects:
Pugh + Scarpa
Principal in charge:
Lawrence Scarpa, AIA
Project team:
Peter Borrego, Angela Brooks AIA, Silke Clemens, Heather Duncan, Vanessa Hardy, Ching Luk, Fredrik Nilsson, Gwynne Pugh AIA, Lawrence Scarpa, Katrin Terstegen
Engineering:
Gordon Polon
General Contractor:
Minardos Inc, George Minardos
Costs:
504000 $
Surface:
520 sqm (5600 sqft)

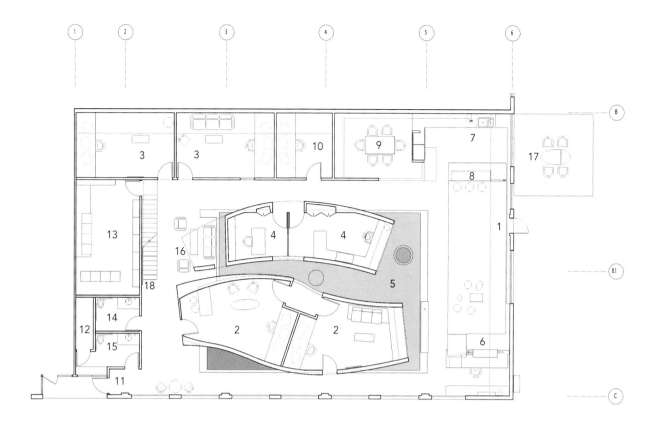

1. Entry
2. Editing studio
3. Editing bay
4. Office
5. Reflecting pool
6. Reception
7. Kitchen
8. Kitchen island - bar
9. Conference room

10. Music studio
11. Service entry
12. Mechanical
13. Library - server
14. Men's bath
15. Women's bath
16. Client waiting - group meeting
17. Patio garden
18. Mezzanine loft above

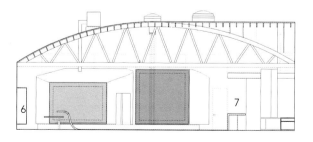

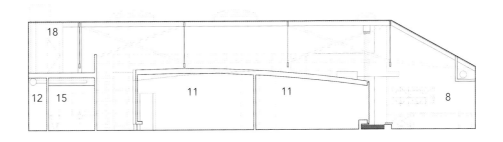

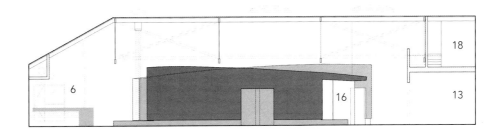

The variety of informal spaces incorporated in the design allows clients and staff to have spaces to relax and to socialize. In addition, the entire entrance zone acts as a café that facilitates informal meetings and client interaction. Social activity is thrown into the limelight. On the opposite side of the café is the reception area, growing out of the linoleum floor material. The reception desk is deliberately moved from the entrance door, encouraging the visitor to absorb the space freely immediately.

The central design elements are the two oblong skewed boxes that enclose the editing studios and offices. Facing the lobby, the ends present a luminous textured façade, which are revealed on closer inspection to be panels filled respectively with ping-pong balls and acrylic beads. While their materials are unorthodox, the functional result is akin to an Arabic filigreed screen. Bathing the rooms in softly diffused light, they afford the users privacy and minimize distractions while allowing glimpses of the space beyond.

The interstices created by the volumes undulating over the shimmering plane of water evoke Venetian canals and Richard Serra's torqued ellipses. A discreet circular "fountain" sunk into the pool fills the space with the soothing sound of running water.

Simone Micheli

Simone Micheli Studio

Florence, Italy

Photographs:
Maurizio Marcato

Architects:
Simone Micheli
Surface:
400 sqm (4300 sqft)
Date:
2005

The original fifteenth century construction, comprised of ample spaces with stone floors, high wooden ceilings and masonry walls, presented a fascinating starting point for this restoration. The project generated a juxtaposition of the new with the old creating a dialogue which is both harmonious and full of contrasts. The intention was to create a fluid environment to host the architectural studio of Simone Micheli.

The spaces created by this ambitious restoration project are: the reception area, waiting room/archive, meeting room, bathroom, project development area, graphics office, and Micheli's office/meeting room.

The totemic cylindrical volume of the reception area welcomes the visitor, completely covered in laminate digital print representing the macro-image of a salad. This bizarre feature forms a sharp contrast with the stone floor, white walls and floor to ceiling cupboard finished in gloss black laminate and shiny stainless steel handles.

The black bathroom also serves as a punchy counterpoint to the brightly colored cylinder. The rectangular "Block" toilets are the only hint of white within this small space. A rectangular steel crack in the mirror serves as the source for air, soap and water, all controlled by electronic sensors.

Adjacent to the reception area is the large central space of the archive and waiting room, which conserves the original structure of the walls and large beams of the ceiling. Black rectangular seats alternate with similar volumes in laminated white that serve as tables. The large white metal filing cupboard is also located here. The adjoining project development area consists of two large rooms connected via an arched opening. The plaster walls, wooden ceilings, shelves and tables for the computers are all white with floors of industrial cement.

At the end of the passageway is Micheli's office/-meeting room. The shelves here are surfaced in shiny white laminate with steel supports and there is a central table with wheels laminated with a colorful design. One of the walls has a mirrored surface, behind which is a small bathroom. The graphics office is decorated with a giant photograph in laminate that covers the entire wall.

The lighting throughout the space is particularly sophisticated making use of incandescent lamps and halogen, led and theatrical lighting to emphasize each and every detail. Large windows on the building's façade allow passers-by to catch a glimpse of these intriguing interiors.

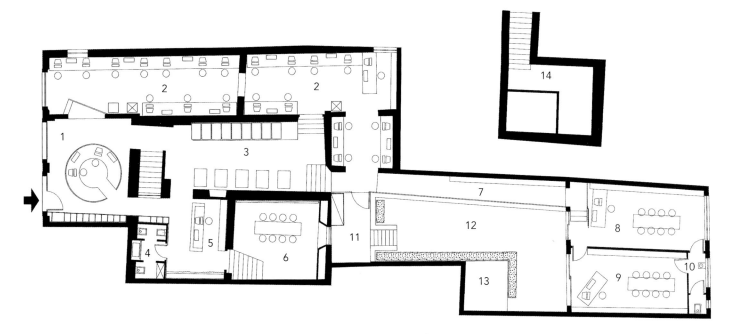

1. Entrance - secretary
2. Project area
3. Waiting area - archive
4. Toilets
5. Secretary
6. Meeting room
7. Corridor
8. Graphics office
9. Micheli´s office - meeting room
10. Toilet
11. Courtyard
12. Garden
13. Technical
14. Archive

A path running alongside a glass wall next to the garden and theatrically lit by a line of blue led lights leads to Micheli's office/meeting room and the graphics office.

The totemic cylindrical volume of the reception area welcomes the visitor, completely covered in laminate digital print representing the macro-image of a salad. This bizarre feature forms a sharp contrast with the stone floor, white walls and floor to ceiling cupboard finished in gloss black laminate and shiny stainless steel handles.

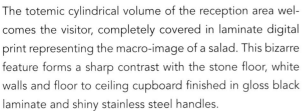

Adjacent to the reception area is the large central space of the archive and waiting room, which conserves the original structure of the walls and large beams of the ceiling. Black rectangular seats alternate with similar volumes in laminated white that serve as tables. The large white metal filing cupboard is also located here.

The suggestive meeting room, located at the foot of a small flight of stairs, which lead from the reception area, is characterized by a white central table and cushioned chairs designed by the architect himself. The walls and vaulted ceiling display rough stone and brick work, highlighted by the unique lighting system which radiates from behind the mirrored wall creating unusual reflections.

The window that looks onto the street is engraved with Simone Micheli's project philosophy.

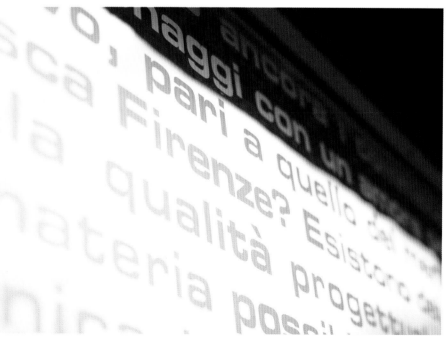

rehauwork

Rehau, Germany

Photographs:
Marcus Weidlich

Rehauwork is a project that addresses the refurbishment of an obsolete but solid industrial building into office space for 150 employees. The existing building could not be altered as it is a listed architectural landmark. The intervention involved inserting all of the modern facilities into the existing structure without affecting it in any way other than restoring it to its original condition. The history of the place is the source of the new intervention. The lofty appearance of the century-old industrial shell with its great window surfaces has been conserved. Based on the colors white and grey, a reductionist material concept developed, permitting porcelain, the product of the enterprise, to speak for itself. The scarce presence of color defines areas, with accents of orange, details of yellow and/or plants.

The architectural work of Michael Weber and Klaus Würschinger, carried out from their offices in Berlin and Weiden, is fundamentally conceptual, stressing comprehensive service to their clients. Besides the basic design they see the development of their projects through to the end. The full integration of all aspects of a project and their wide range of experience and capacity to work in with the wide variety of professionals involved enable weber+würschinger to deliver powerfully satisfactory results.

They have been associated with urban designers, landscape architects and engineers, a full range of supporting skills that underpins their work in overall planning. An important branch of their activities is corporate architecture: the successful symbiosis between architecture, interior design and design provides responsive service for corporate clients, who seek to use their installations to represent their firm's philosophy and culture. Their guiding principle is in-depth dialogue with the clients that defines all the qualifications of a project. A methodical examination of all the factors enables the concept to be developed step by step. In urban planning, one of their strong points is the attention granted to geographical conditions. New buildings are envisaged not as isolated phenomena, self contained autonomous units, but as interventions by which the qualities of an environment or a public space may be positively influenced. By closely linking layout, design and materials, the charm of their buildings is not grandiloquent details but clear, high quality functionalism that results from solid concepts. Many different solutions are weighed and considered in order to control investment costs while ensuring constructive quality and architectural expression. The search for cost-conscious production processes involves an active collaboration with all the partners from the project's earliest planning stage.

Architects:
weber+würschinger
Gesellschaft von Architekten
mbH
Project partner:
Haye Bakker
Construction managment:
weber+würschinger with
REHAU AG+Co
Structure engineer:
Schneider und Partner
Ingenieur Consult GmbH
Mechanical engineer:
REHAU AG+Co
Acoustics:
Ingenieurbüro Leistner
Lighting design:
weber+würschinger with
Lichtberater Jürgen Faatz
Surface:
3200 sqm (34 430 sqft)

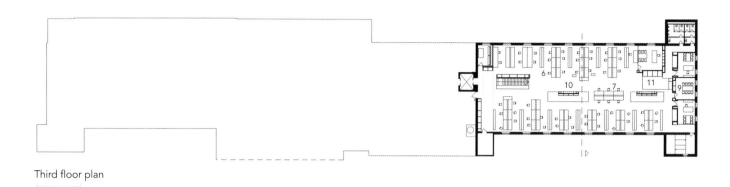

Third floor plan

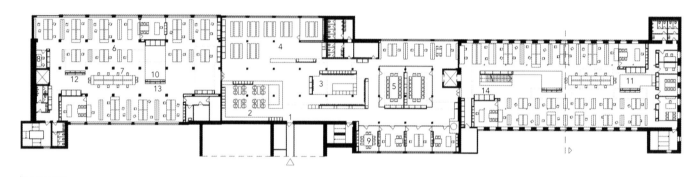

Second floor plan

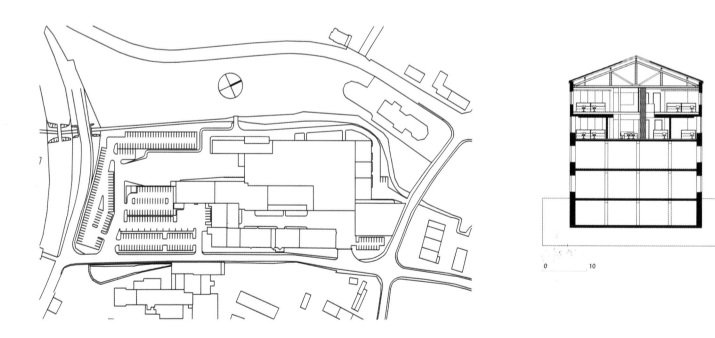

1. Entrance
2. Lounge
3. Exhibition space
4. Cafeteria
5. Video-conference
6. Permanent workstations
7. Temporary workstations
8. Cockpit
9. Meeting room
10. Copy point
11. Tea point
12. Open meeting place
13. Plant wall
14. Drawing archive

All the floors are made of massive oak planks. The printers and other technical accessories, including storage, are located in the center of each department, in the so-called "functional zones", which create a technical strip throughout the entire center of the building, in accordance with the most recent research developments in workspace-dynamics.

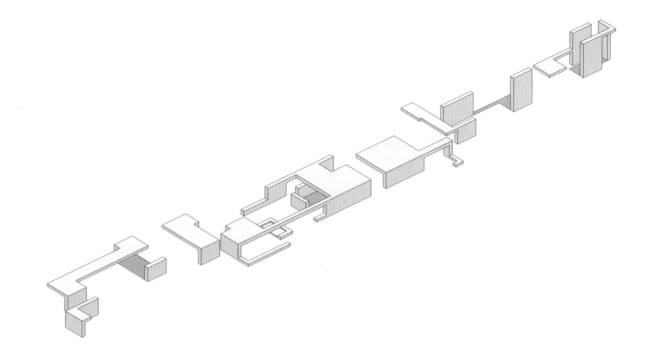

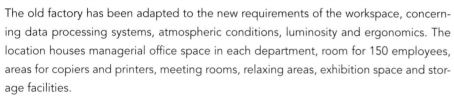

The old factory has been adapted to the new requirements of the workspace, concerning data processing systems, atmospheric conditions, luminosity and ergonomics. The location houses managerial office space in each department, room for 150 employees, areas for copiers and printers, meeting rooms, relaxing areas, exhibition space and storage facilities.

dRMM

Selfridges&Co

London, UK

Photographs:
Alex de Rijke

In 2001, the discerning former CEO of Selfridges, Vittorio Radice, commissioned dRMM to design a new VIP entrance, staff offices and a 'buyers' lounge' for international fashion designers showing new collections. The brief required a mid-term solution that would be reworked after several seasons. Inserted within an office building incorporated behind the main Oxford Street Selfridges store, the refurbished interior is mostly on the top (fourth) floor.

A new Duke Street ground floor entrance is both welcoming and intriguing to the visitor outside. A graduating matrix of white dots on full height sheets of glass, superimposed on top of the listed building stonework, reveals glimpses of the lobby beyond. This helps distinguish the VIP entrance from the Selfridges store, but offers a distinct marker for the behind the scene activities. The lobby interior is a pause in transit; purposefully understated with a white seamless resin floor/wall finish, punctuated only by the reception and lift entrances. All is simply defined by shape, light and reflection.

The spectacular buyers' lounge on the top floor is an informal meeting space, arranged as a fluid wrap of 3D elastic screen walls around a resin coffee bar. The plan allows those working there to pass through discreetly, and those doing business there to soak up the office atmosphere while finding privacy and refreshment. A smaller meeting room is defined by perforated concave 'wrap' wall. The combination of a limited palette of 'jointless' materials with Lensvelt furniture, make for extraordinary space and light.

Architects:
dRMM (de Rijke Marsh Morgan Architects)
Structural Engineering:
Michael Hadi Associates
Contractor:
Barnwood Shopfitters
Client:
Selfridges&Co
Total floor area:
298 sqm (3200 sqft)
Project duration:
2001 – 2007

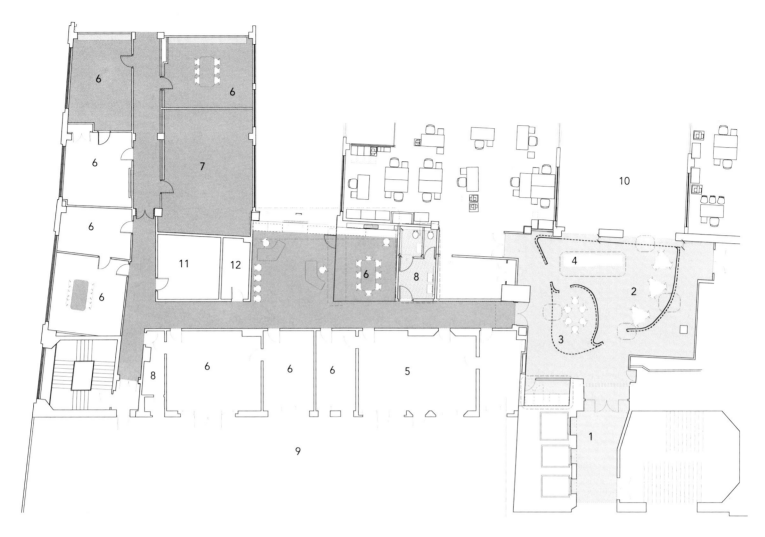

GA Plan: Fourth floor

1. Lift lobby
2. Buyers' lounge
3. Meeting area
4. Coffee bar
5. Board room
6. Office
7. Meeting room
8. Toilet
9. Terrace
10. Light well
11. Comms room
12. Kitchen

 Existing

Designed by dRMM

A new Duke Street ground floor entrance is both welcoming and intriguing to the visitor outside. A graduating matrix of white dots on full height sheets of glass, superimposed on top of the listed building stonework, reveals glimpses of the lobby beyond.

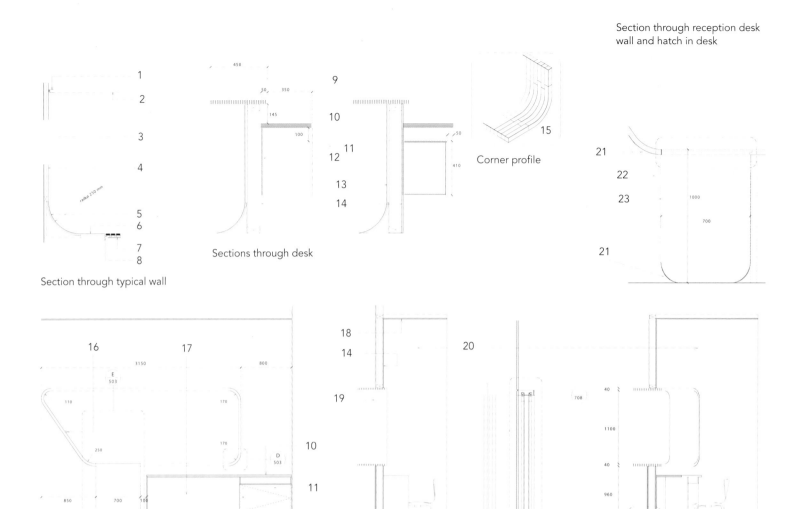

Section through reception desk
wall and hatch in desk

Section through typical wall

Corner profile

Sections through desk

View of desk from behind

Sections

1. Barrisol clip screw fixed to wall
2. Barrisol ceiling
3. Wall panels 18 mm plywood,
4. Altrotect resin to floor and walls
5. Plywood coving formed from 18 mm plywood to base and back with 2 × 6 mm flexiply screwed and glued to edges of formers giving profile
6. 18 mm plywood screw fixed to concrete floor
7. "Street-beater" Black ribbed rubber/silver alu. 22 mm gauge approx
8. 31.7 × 25.4 × 3.2 mm aluminium angle
9. 24 mm birch ply cut into 40 mm deep strips and laminated together. Spray laquered (clear)
10. Balanced yellow laminate on 18 mm birch ply
11. Lockable storage cupboard
12. 18 mm birch ply carcass, spray laquered (clear)
13. Altrotect resin on 18 mm plywood fixed to timber stud wall

14. 12 mm plasterboard, skimmed and painted traffic white RAL 9016
15. Routed curve plywood profiles laminated together and finger jointed with straight sections
16. 2 no. allgood d-line wall stop with black rubber buffer, 14 mm dia.
17. 18mm birch ply, countersunk screwed to wall finish: spray laquered
18. Reception ceiling 50 × 100 sw joists at 400 c/c using continuous m/s angle bolted to masonry wall.
19. 24 mm birch ply cut into 40 mm deep strips and laminated together as end grain sheet. Corners: routed curved profile laminated together.
20. 12 mm plasterboard, skimmed and painted rape yellow RAL 1021
21. Softwood shaped to form profile for opening
22. 50 × 100 mm timber stud wall
23. Hatchway opening lined with 3 mm brushed stainless steel bonded to timber joists and floor buildup

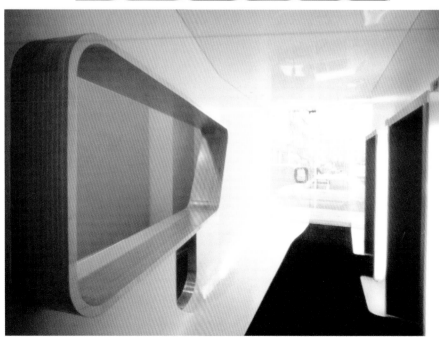

The spectacular buyer's lounge on the top floor is an informal meeting space, arranged as a fluid wrap of 3D elastic screen walls around a resin coffee bar. The plan allows those working there to pass through discreetly, and those doing business there to soak up the office atmosphere while finding privacy and refreshment.

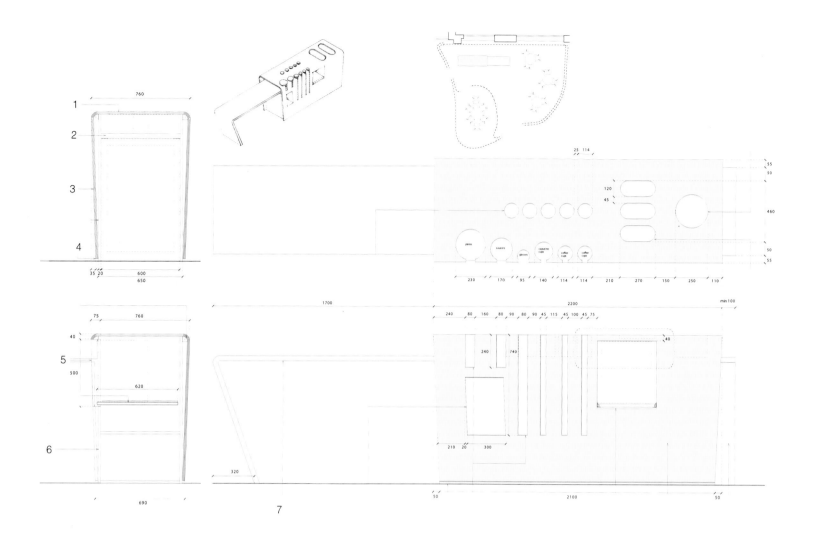

1. Altrotect resin to all exposed surfaces of flexi MDF counter top
2. 2 layers of 18 mm plywood forming worktop with 2 mm brushed stainless steel clad to exposed faces
3. 3 layers of 6 mm flexi MDF folded over plywood frame forming coffee bar counter and sides
4. 18 mm plywood forming interior carcass with 2 mm brushed stainless steel clad to exposed faces
5. 20 × 20 mm brushed stainless steel angle
6. 40 × 40 mm softwood fixed to plywood carcass and shaped to form round corner to counter top edge. radius approx. 30 mm
7. 3 mm brushed stainless steel pieces cladd to top, base and side faces of opening for coffee maker
8. Sliding brushed stainless steel shelf for coffee maker fixed to plywood side panels on base mounting stainless steel Haeffle drawer runners
9. 18mm plywood carcass forming frame for flexi MDF
10. 5 × 114 mm brushed s/s tube with s/s flat welded to base forming container

11. Brushed s/s welded to form container tray. Hole cut into counter top with chamfered edges to match tray
12. 2 layers of 18 mm plywood forming worktop and leg with 2 mm brushed stainless steel clad to exposed faces and edges
13. 3 mm brushed s/s flat welded to form carcass for tray shelf fitted within plywood carcass
14. 2100 × 20 × 20 mm brushed s/s angle to full length of counter base
15. Holder for plates, cups and glasses formed from brushed s/s tube with s/s flat welded to base giving a container and fixed within plywood carcass. Sections cut into length forming opening and giving access to chinawear.
16. Opening for coffee maker with exposed edged lined with 3 mm brushed s/s. Brushed s/s sliding shelf fixed to plywood side panels on base mounting stainless steel Haeffle drawer runners
17. Altrotect resin on 3 layers of 6 mm flexi MDF and folded over plywood frame forming coffee bar counter
18. 18 mm plywood side panels to fridge clad with 2 mm brushed s/s to exposed faces & edges

RO&AD architecten

A Cardboard suit for Scherpontwerp

Eindhoven, The Netherlands

Photographs:
Anita Huisman

Architects:
RO&AD architecten,
Ro Koster, Ad Kil

In planning a new office space for their clients Scherpontwerp, a graphic design company and De Boekenmakers, publishers, in the centre of Eindhoven in The Netherlands, RO&AD Architects drew inspiration surprisingly from the open spaces of Central Park in Manhattan. In their view it is a good example of a clear space, defined by a rectangle where no buildings are allowed. Their objective was to convert 200 sqm (2150 sqft) of dreary, disorganised rented office space into a pleasant and stimulating working environment within a limited budget.

They applied the urban concept as seen in Central Park to the office environment. First they defined the maximum rectangular space in the centre of the area, then filled the outer edges with cardboard. The functional items needed - shelves, desks, work stations, meeting areas, a canteen and walk-in cupboards - were then sculpted out of the cardboard, while a long low table was created out of cardboard in the central area. Just as the buildings around Central Park define the park, the interior cardboard edges define the open space in this office; the buildings have urban functions and the interior facades have interior functions.

Initial doubts about the practicality and aesthetics of working in this environment made out of honeycomb cardboard were soon resolved as it became clear that it is a sound-absorbent material so reduces noise levels, creating a peaceful working habitat. Furthermore it is a pleasing material which lends a certain warmth to the office and the large-scale repetition of the striped pattern contributes to the peace and uniformity of the space.

There is also a pragmatic element in this scheme which meets the clients' brief. Architects Ad Kil and Ro Koster comment that they could not achieve what the client required with conventional building materials as the budget was 30 % too low. Cardboard is light, relatively cheap, easy to work with and transport and available in different kinds of thickness and finishes. It only took four months to build using nothing but glue. Furthermore the lease for the space will run out after five years so a more permanent material would be wasted and as fashions in office design are bound to change the current fittings can happily be dumped in the recycling bin.

Although the interior may look like a house of cards it is as strong as concrete and can withstand a certain amount of wear and tear. Horizontal joists give the table strength but if it gets damaged it will not be a huge investment to make another.

As a final poetic word it is very fitting that a publisher and design company who work with paper and make a living from it should now be working literally within a paper-based interior.

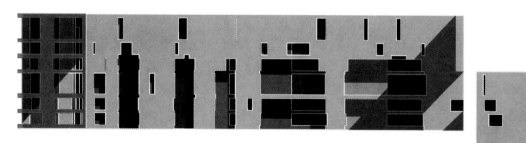

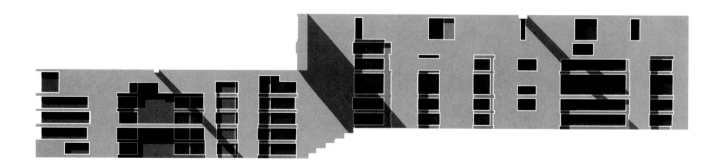

The architects applied the urban concept as seen in Central Park to the office environment. First they defined the maximum rectangular space in the centre of the area, then filled the outer edges with cardboard. Just as the buildings around Central Park define the park, the interior cardboard edges define the open space in this office; the buildings have urban functions and the interior facades have interior functions.

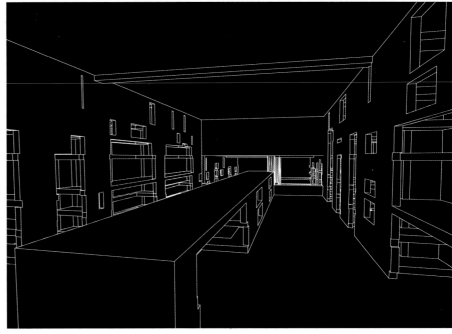

Initial doubts about the practicality and aesthetics of working in this environment made out of honeycomb cardboard were soon resolved as it became clear that it is a sound-absorbent material so reduces noise levels, creating a peaceful working habitat.

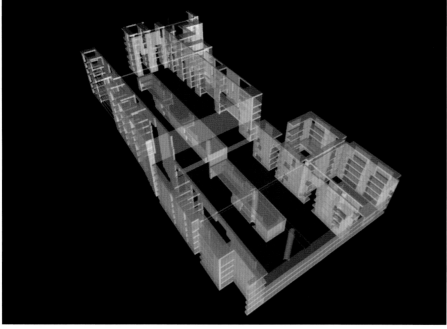

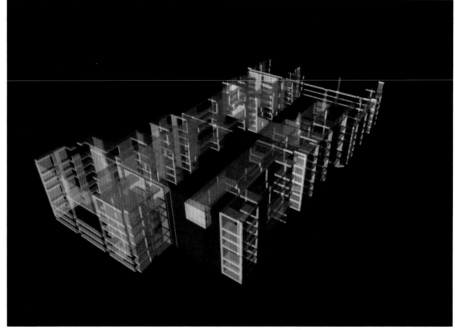

It only took four months to build using nothing but glue. Furthermore the lease for the space will run out after five years so a more permanent material would be wasted and as fashions in office design are bound to change the current fittings can happily be dumped in the recycling bin.

Although the interior may look like a house of cards it is as strong as concrete and can withstand a certain amount of wear and tear. Horizontal joists give the table strength but if it gets damaged it will not be a huge investment to make another.

Grip Limited

Toronto, Canada

Photographs:
Tom Arban

Architects:

Johnson Chou Inc

Project team:

Silke Stadtmueller,

Mark Ojascastro, Bryan Jin,

Phil Cates, Ronen Bauer,

Johnson Chou

This is Johnson Chou's second project for the Canadian advertising agency, Grip, whose original space was located above Caban on Queen West. The plans for the new offices incorporated an array of different spaces into the building's first, fifth and sixth floors. The resulting space included a reception area, formal and creative boardrooms, meeting rooms, an atrium, creative offices, open workstations, studio spaces, kitchens, a lunch area, lounges, rooms for screening, editing, and photography and showers.

The essential question Johnson Chou's design team had to answer was how to express creativity within the lexicon of architecture. The three aims the designers needed to fulfil when planning the project were: firstly, to create a collection of formal and informal meeting spaces throughout the agency, which inspire and foster creativity for those working there; secondly, to make the journeys between these spaces enjoyable, thereby conveying to clients and visitors that they are first and foremost a creative agency; and finally to manifest the notion of play and wit, pertinent in the original space, paralleling the uniqueness of the agency's creative work. The resulting space is highly innovative, in keeping with the company's reputation.

An atrium visually and functionally links the two main floors, the fifth and sixth, with a double-height space, within which the major gathering/lounging activities and vertical circulation take place. A staircase here relates to the bleacher seating, constructed from folded, hot-rolled steel and stained walnut veneer. This provides a gathering space for full office meetings, film presentations and an alternative workplace with a laptop. Vertical circulation is also provided by way of a slide, which has become the adopted symbol at Grip, and a fire-pole, which both connect the creative offices located on the two levels at the north wall. These surprisingly exhilarating and unique experiences of movement through the office act as a metaphor for the agency's belief in the importance of the creative process; a methodology centered on the notion that the journey is as important as the destination, and should be as enjoyable.

The meeting/lounge area was designed to resemble a hot tub capable of seating ten people. This small pool offers a circular (and therefore democratic) seating format, and has often been used to disarm the most difficult of clients.

A more formal boardroom, known as "the fridge", makes reference to Grip's beer industry clients. Clad in stainless steel, the interior is finished with white synthetic grass, used to absorb sound and because of its resemblance to frost.

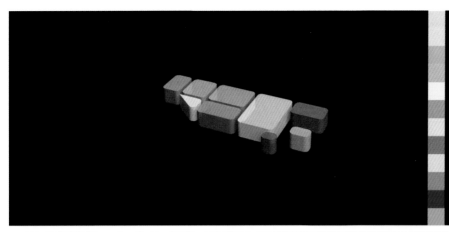

Reception
Creative offices
Meeting rooms
Kitchen
Open offices
Library
Studio
Atrium
Gallery
Screenin rooms
Editing and photo rooms
Shower, lockers

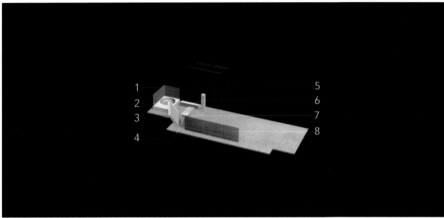

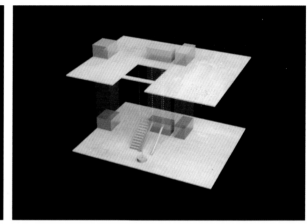

Ground floor

1. Presentation wall
2. Hot-tub
3. Art wall
4. Entrance "tube"

5. Screening rooms
6. Kitchen
7. "Orange Ice" lunch area
8. Mirror wall

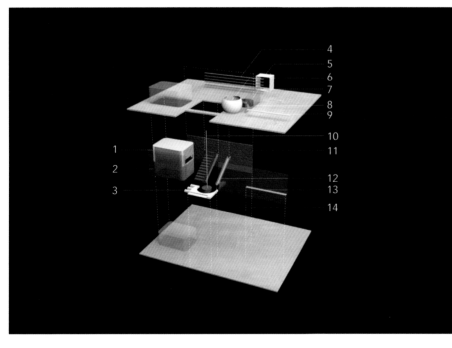

Fifth and sixth floors

1. "The Fridge" main boardroom
2. Creative boardroom
3. "Landscaped" area
4. Library
5. "Ice Cube" meeting room
6. Reception "pod"
7. Reception desk
8. Orange glass wall
9. Floating light table
10. Fire pole and cushion
11. Felt wall
12. Slide
13. Floating light table
14. Creative offices, mirror wall

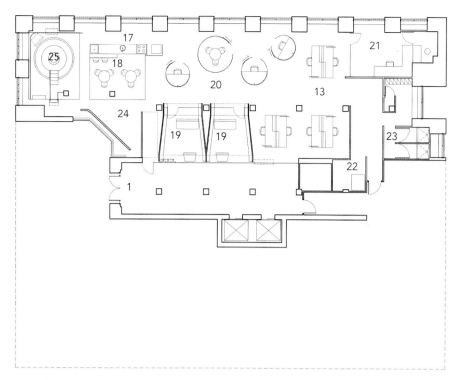

Ground floor plan

The meeting/lounge area was designed to resemble a hot tub capable of seating ten people. This small pool offers a circular (and therefore democratic) seating format, and has often been used to disarm the most difficult of clients.

1. Building lobby
2. Reception
3. Waiting
4. Formal boardroom
5. Creative boardroom
6. Atrium
7. Bleacher seating
8. Slide
9. Bridge
10. Fire pole
11. Lounge
12. Creative offices
13. Open workstations
14. Studio area
15. Partners' workstations
16. Meeting room
17. Kitchen
18. Lunch area
19. Screening room
20. Meeting / work pod
21. Editing room
22. Photography studio
23. Showers
24. Art wall
25. "Hot-tub"
26. Library

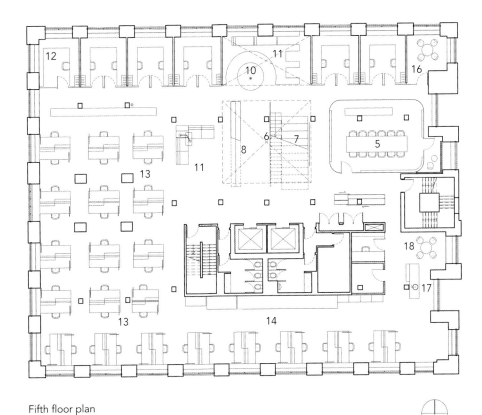

Fifth floor plan

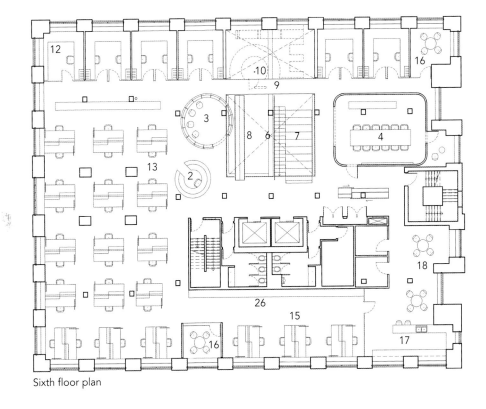

Sixth floor plan

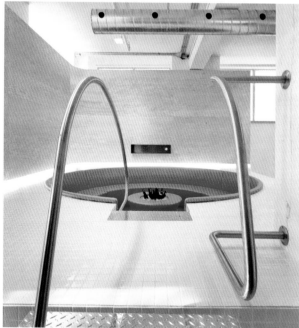

The formal boardroom, known as "the fridge", makes reference to one of Grip's clients, a beer company. Clad in stainless steel, the interior is finished with white synthetic grass, used to absorb sound and because of its resemblance to frost.

HLW

HBO

Los Angeles, California, USA

Photographs:
Benny Chan / Fotoworks

Architects:
HLW
Project team:
Chari Jalali, Kevin Kilmer,
Susie Tin Liang,
Deb Longua-Zamero,
Sarah Qing Mei,
Gerard Roberts, David Swartz,
Christy Wallace,
Mavis Wiggins, Silva Zeitlian
Technical consultant:
Plan Net Consulting
Structural engineers:
Structural Focus
Acoustical engineers:
Charles M. Salter Associates
Mechanical engineers:
Syska Hennessy Group
General contractor:
Inner Space Constructors
Client:
HBO
Total surface:
10 230 sqm (110 000 sqft)

This space is a two floor, 10 230 sqm (110 000 sqft) office space for an entertainment client, which includes special program elements such as a screening room to seat thirty people, a two level prefunction / reception lobby with an enormous skylight, a high density film vault, and edit bays. The primary challenge was to design a space that reflected the client's culture, which had been broken down into four basic characteristics: classic and innovative, scaled to the individual, sense of humor and surprise, and unique perspectives.

The design of the workstations draws on the design of a classic walnut desk from the fifties with the innovative addition of a colored resin material as the inset for the desk top material. This is similar to the traditional leather "blotter", yet it is also fresh and unique. In the long corridor separating the elevator lobby from the reception area is a concrete floor with handprints from the employees, allowing them to leave their permanent mark of individuality on the space. Features such as the enormous domed light fixture in the reception lobby afford a sense of surprise to an otherwise sophisticated space. It was established that the company works best when they take a fairly typical subject and look at it with a unique perspective. In this vein, the element of a "ticker tape", which people are used to seeing every day in a horizontal format, was turned to run vertically so it appears to cut through the floor slab.

To allow natural light to reach such deep floor plates, a 10 × 20 m (30 × 60 ft) skylight has been installed in the reception lobby that bathes both floors in light. Three further additional skylights were included over gathering nodes connecting both floors along the circulation pathways. The space has been laid out in such a way that it enables the executive team to work closely, yet also allows them to be close to the groups they manage. An "executive pod" was created at the center of the floor plates with an interconnecting executive stair and each of their groups fan out from their office in a "pie" shape.

Sustainable materials such as designing all of the case goods in the offices with a bamboo veneer instead of wood, meet the client's environmentally conscious premises.

In order to encourage interaction amongst employees, along the "shortcut" pathways that cut through the space, gathering nodes were added with pantry bars, flat screen TV's, lounge seating, and skylights above. To the same end, large sliding "barnyard" doors were designed for the offices, opening them more to the workstations and allowing natural light to enter. In keeping with the company's character "a sense of humor and surprise" was injected by subtly etching the company logo onto a huge wide glass screen behind the reception desk. A large billboard to display current releases was printed on a mesh material that you can see through from the boardroom down into the reception area.

Fourth floor plan

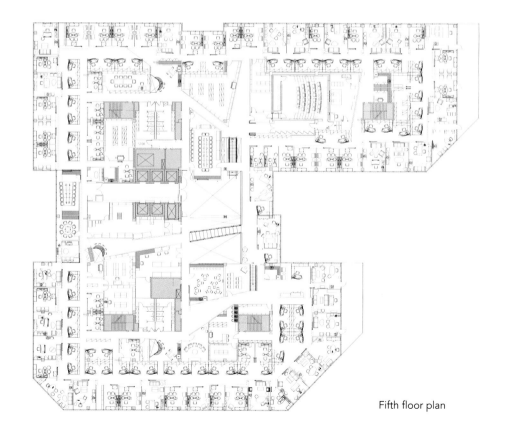

Fifth floor plan

In keeping with the company's character "a sense of humor and surprise" was injected by subtly etching the company logo onto a huge wide glass screen behind the reception desk. A large billboard to display current releases was printed on a mesh material that you can see through from the boardroom down into the reception area.

Features such as the enormous domed light fixture in the reception lobby afford a sense of surprise to an otherwise sophisticated space.

The design of the workstations draws on the design of a classic walnut desk from the fifties with the innovative addition of a colored resin material as the inset for the desk top material. This is similar to the traditional leather "blotter", yet it is also fresh and unique.

Mario Cucinella Architects

Uniflair

Conselve, Italy

Photographs:
**Jean de Calan,
Marco Covi**

The Uniflair project consists of a twofold intervention: the first part concerns the landscape, envisaged as a patchwork that contaminates the predominantly industrial character of the area. As the location is in the country, the intention was to avoid transmitting the notion that industry is "stealing space from the landscape". Hence the addition of pleasingly ambiguous elements, that disrupt the uniform grayness of cement and asphalt: areas paved with red tinted concrete, trees scattered irregularly, to look as though they were already there, and green areas, such as a bamboo garden and a flower-strewn field.

The second part of the intervention concerns the interior layout of the building allocated to the technical offices. The interior is a 200 m (650 ft) long open plan structure where the various workplaces are brought together along one single table that stretches in a continuous line through the entire space, a visible backbone that is an explicit representation of company procedures. The space is lit by a system of indirect lighting positioned in the central part of the table. Next to the long table a series of cylindrical spaces provide meeting rooms, areas for relaxing, and communal areas. They look like circular pavilions and are lit from inside.

In clear contrast with the linear layout of the industrial process, these spaces create a new interior landscape, designed with the idea of eliminating all physical barriers between the different activities, yet guaranteeing the necessary degree of privacy for work to proceed in comfort. Thus, a lighting system was devised that would be integrated into that of the main work space. The pavilions represent mere circular screens suspended from the ceiling, that air, light and sounds can go through. The material chosen for the walls of these modules is a relatively experimental type of plastic with a particular molecular structure making it outstandingly sound-absorbing. Generally used for backlit double ceilings, it provides the degree of privacy required while transforming each meeting room into a lantern in the full sense of the word.

Architects:

Mario Cucinella Architects

Project team:

Mario Cucinella,
Elizabeth Francis,
Tommaso Bettini (responsible),
Giulio Altieri, Eva Cantwell,
Carmine Concas,
Davide Paolini

Structural engineer:

Giuseppe Cecinato

Client:

Uniflair Industries Spa

Gross floor area:

3600 sqm (38700 sqft)

▲Marco Covi

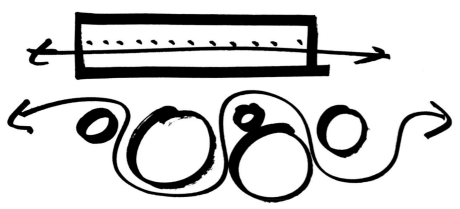

As the location is in the country, the intention was to avoid transmitting the notion that industry is "stealing space from the landscape". Hence the addition of pleasant items far removed from the uniform grayness of cement and asphalt: areas in red tinted concrete, trees scattered so as to seem pre-existing, and green areas, such as a bamboo garden and a flower-strewn field.

Jean de Calan ▲

Efficient use and control of natural light has been obtained by means of closely-woven blinds mounted on rollers and cables outside the building, with a wind-sensitive and light-sensitive mechanism that regulates the angle – greater or lesser – of the openings.

▼ Jean de Calan

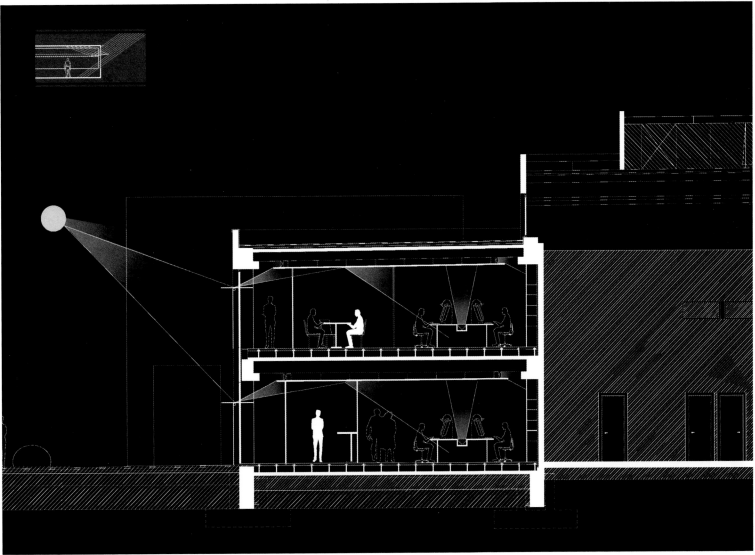

Jean de Calan ▼

Jean de Calan ◄▲►

◀▲ Marco Covi

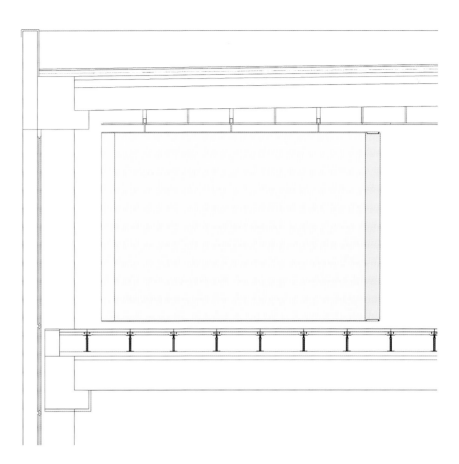

Contradicting the linear industrial layout, the meeting room modules create a new interior landscape. Designed to eliminate physical barriers between different activities, they guarantee the privacy needed for work to proceed in comfort. The pavilions represent mere circular screens suspended from the ceiling, that air, light and sounds can go through. The walls of these modules consist of a new plastic with outstanding sound-absorbing and light-permeable properties. Each meeting room is a lantern.

▲▼▶ Jean de Calan

The interior is a 200 m long open plan structure where the various workplaces are brought together along one single table that stretches in a continuous line through the entire space, a visible backbone that is an explicit representation of company procedures. The space is lit by a system of indirect lighting positioned in the central part of the table.

Bureaux-Habitation, Gand

Sint – Denijs – Westrem, Belgium

Photographs:
Vercruysse & Dujardin

The Belgian team of architects 'NU architectuuratelier' has transformed this site, which previously hosted a mid-century bungalow, into an office/house. Erected on the foundations of the previous building, the present development was required to have an ambivalent function. It was to be an advertising agency today with scope for conversion into housing in the future. The client demanded an infinite list of possible future functions and applications to be incorporated in the design. This called for an open and flexible layout.

The building stands in an area which is subject to early floods, and has therefore been placed on a white concrete plinth that forms both a literal and metaphorical island. Above the pedestal is a complex form whose character is neither recognizably commercial nor domestic. The black sculpture is reminiscent of a modern villa, yet the north-light roof construction has the character of industrial architecture. Daylight enters not only through four north-light roofs, creating a diffused lighting mood in the white internal space, but also through four large areas of glazing, each and every one positioned at the end of a wall. The entrance façade is entirely glazed allowing light to flood into the interior. The skylights and enormous windows accentuate the dimensions of the internal space, and generate a strong connection between the interior and the exterior. In this environment the simple and austere furnishings, designed by the architects, have their own restrained effect. One flat-roofed corner of the rectangular 11 by 20 meter (33 by 60 foot) building is screened from the main area and comprises the serving space. This contains the bathroom and the kitchen. Every detail, from the zinc cladding to the joints in the concrete floor, is handled with the same intensity.

Concealed behind the zinc cladding is a steel-reinforced timber post-and-rail structure. The skin of the building is characterized by very refined detailing across the complex geometry. The detailing and geometry applied does not only control the physical and structural characteristics, but also especially the aesthetics of the building. The use of natural materials (concrete, steel, aluminum, black zinc, wood) supports the timeless and monolithical character of the building.

Architects:
NU architectuuratelier
Project team:
Arlauskas Arunas,
Eeckels Armand
Realisation:
2005
Surface:
186 sqm (2000 sqft)

The skin of the building is characterized by very refined detailing across the complex geometry. The detailing and geometry applied does not only control the physical and structural characteristics, but also especially the aesthetics of the building. The use of natural materials (concrete, steel, aluminum, black zinc, wood) supports the timeless and monolithical character of the building.

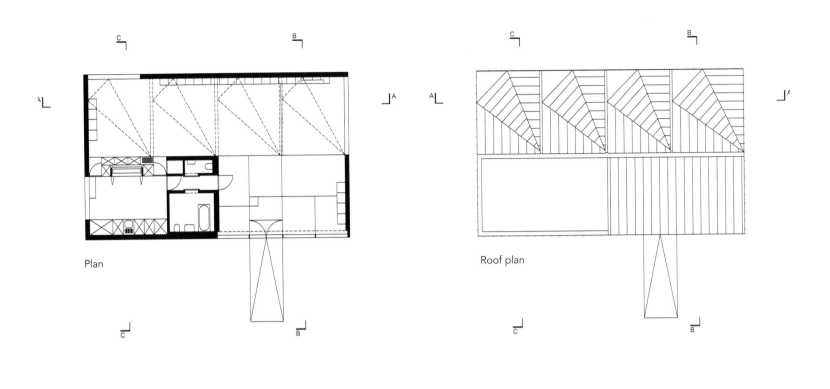

Plan

Roof plan

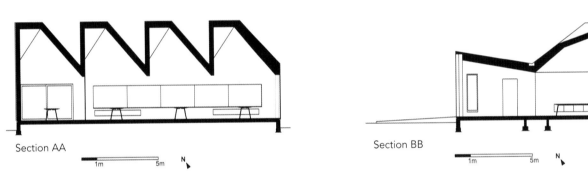

Section AA

1m   5m   N

Section BB

1m   5m   N

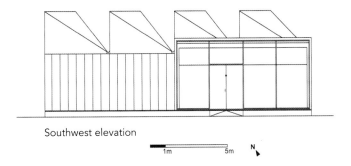

Southwest elevation

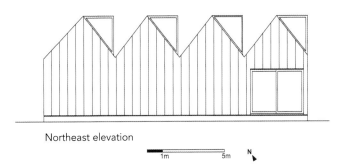

Northeast elevation

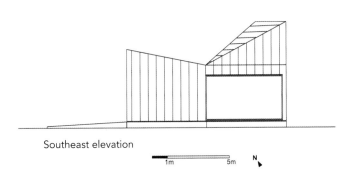

Southeast elevation

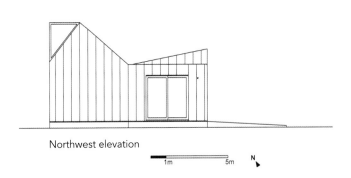

Northwest elevation

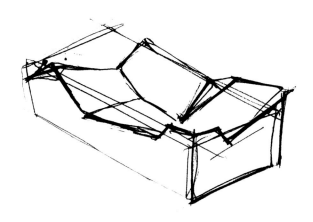

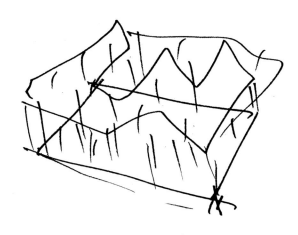

Daylight enters not only through four north-light roofs, creating a diffused lighting mood in the white internal space, but also through four large areas of glazing, each and every one positioned at the end of a wall.

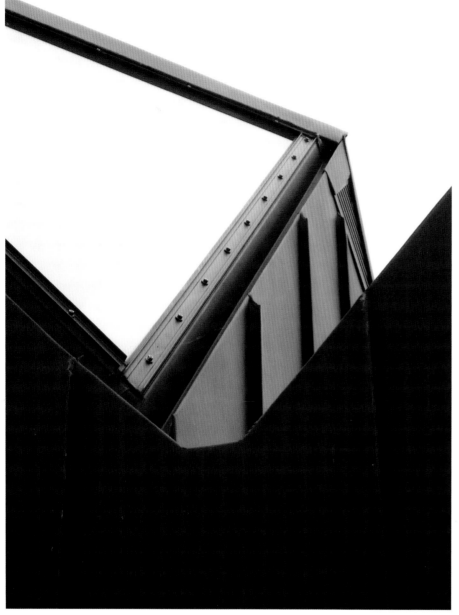

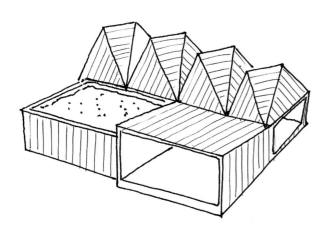

The skylights and enormous windows accentuate the dimensions of the internal space, and generate a strong connection between the interior and the exterior. In this environment the simple and austere furnishings, designed by the architects, have their own restrained effect.

René González Architect

KARLA Conceptual Event Experiences

Miami, Florida, USA

Photographs:
Ken Hayden

Having seen work by René González at a design exhibition, Karla Dascal, founder of event organizing business, Karla Conceptual Event Experiences, decided to commission the architect to design a venue to host the company's new headquarters in an old warehouse just off Biscayne Boulevard in Miami's trendy Wynwood Arts District. Dascal wanted a minimalist space where clients could be brought to and seduced. A place where they could be inspired, with enough openness to allow their imaginations to fly. The venue would also be used for throwing parties, making TV sets and preparing floral arrangements for catered events.

The site includes a warehouse occupying a surface area of 1120 sqm (12 000 sqft), and an unbuilt adjacent lot, overgrown with vegetation, of the same dimensions. The new building, simply named Karla, was designed with a simple floor plan using innovative material applications. Interior spaces center on two internally lighted acrylic walls fronted by the lobby and reception area. The lobby, conference room, and workspace form a series of high-ceilinged, boxy white spaces, some with these glowing, light-infused walls. The built-in reception desk seems to float above the high-gloss epoxy floor. On the wall behind the desk is finished with handmade, 3D white wallpaper, designed by artist Tracy Kendall. Etched-acrylic and the floor-to-ceiling panels, backlit through blue filters, define the reception area's other edges. All the spaces and fixtures for the project were designed and chosen with simplicity of form and material to maximize effect while staying within a budget. The program also included corporate offices, a flower cooler, and ample storage space. The company's dynamic designers can be viewed creating the events and arrangements through translucent panels, which offers clients a sensation of intimacy once they are inside this serene space. Custom-designed light fixtures, wall finishes and furniture complement the minimal interiors. The result is a silky, luminous space that forms the perfect backdrop for this company.

The property's empty lot was converted into a lush, subtropical garden, which visitors to the building have to traverse in order to enter the structure through its reoriented main entrance. The sequence of landscaped spaces created here can be used for events and ancillary activities. Huge, single-paned glass doors separate the lobby from the garden and heighten ambiguities in the indoor/outdoor relationship.

This remarkable transformation of "undistinguished shell" to "temple of light" provides a huge sense of serenity, as well as the flexibility that a company of this nature requires.

Architect:
René González Architect
Principal in charge:
René González
Project team:
Monica Vázquez
Structural engineer:
Wood and Associates
Mechanical engineer:
Vidal and Associates
Contractor:
Madison Construction
Costs:
1 000 000 $
Surface:
1120 sqm (12 000 sqft)

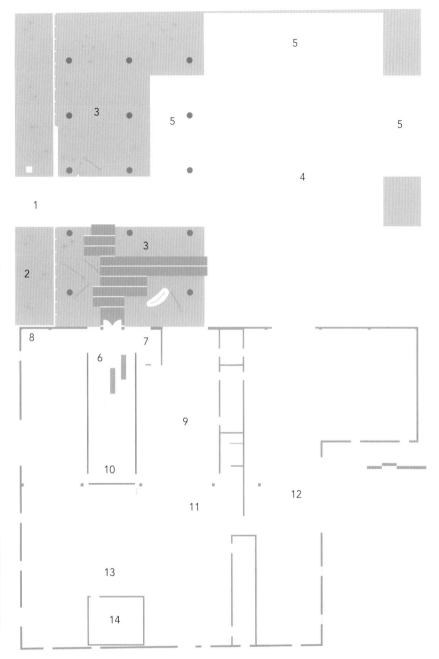

1. Main entry – driveway
2. Corten steel wall
3. Garden
4. Outdoor event space
5. Parking
6. Lobby
7. Reception desk
8. Installation
9. Office space
10. Conference room
11. Executive office
12. Warehouse space
13. Production studio
14. Flower cooler

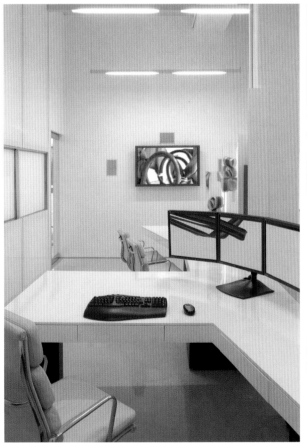

Advertising Agency Terán / TBWA

Lomas de Chapultepec, Mexico D.F., Mexico

Photographs:
Laura Cohen

The first thing that attracted the architects to enter the interior design competition for this advertising agency was their slogan "The idea factory", which gave them incentive to find an unbiased, free flowing proposal. Their proposal caused some controversy since it involved taking the rented building apart, creating a three-story central space and providing access from the elevator on the middle floor by way of a spiral staircase. This created the perfect setting for a free flowing, dynamic interaction.

Once the project was accepted, the designers started to research how the advertising agency functioned. Working in collaboration with Terán, they studied each area and the interaction between them. It was requested that they invent a central element that would lend strength and identity to the agency, using the premise of a "totem pole". Their response was an asymmetrical stack of wooden boxes, with an independent movement and digital screens, to form an element that would vertically penetrate the central opening, communicating and integrating, by way of images and sound, the general mood of the users.

Movement in a creative agency is essential in all its possible interpretations, so all work-related elements have been designed with wheels: desks, chairs, filing cabinets, doors and meeting rooms where ideas are created. The floor was therefore freed of all possible obstructions, and a central, suspended information column was created, with ramifications of information that lead to the brain; the "Site" located in a central area and held in a glass box.

The architects wanted spaces that were open and free of obstacles and designed hidden filing cabinets, using the exterior perimeter of the building's circulation nucleus as storage space, since this area is accessible to all users. It is covered with black doors that also serve as a large blackboard for people to draw on. These combine well with the space, as well as serving to hide the filing cabinets.

Thin walls made from over 23 000 CD\DVD boxes were used to create a space where employees could be by themselves in a "container" of ideas. This space, called "Think Room", alludes to these "digital information containers". When this place is in use, the words "Think Room" lit up.

To create a graphic image that would integrate with the surroundings, all the columns of the building were covered, increasing the apparent size of the building and obtaining "light boxes" that transformed into spontaneous images.

With the client's collaboration and support, a modern workplace was created with personality and its own identity, which would incite individual and group creativity. Without doubt Terán's new "idea factory".

Architects:
Garduño Arquitectos
Juan Garduño, Ernesto Flores, Ricardo Guzmán, Daniel Banda, Athos Sajid
Structural design:
Aguilar engineers, Salvador Aguilar
Construction:
Alen Construcciones, Enrique Alvarez
Installations:
RCL Instalaciones, Roberto Campoy
Furniture:
Vital Design by Actiu, Sillas Herman Miller
Illumination:
Italli Illumination
Client:
Terán / TBWA
Surface area:
2500 sqm (26 900 sqft)
Date:
2005
Awards:
Winner" of the 9th "Architectural Record/Business Week Awards program", 2006. Merit Award at the "XVth Pan-American Architecture Biennial Competition", 2006, in Quito

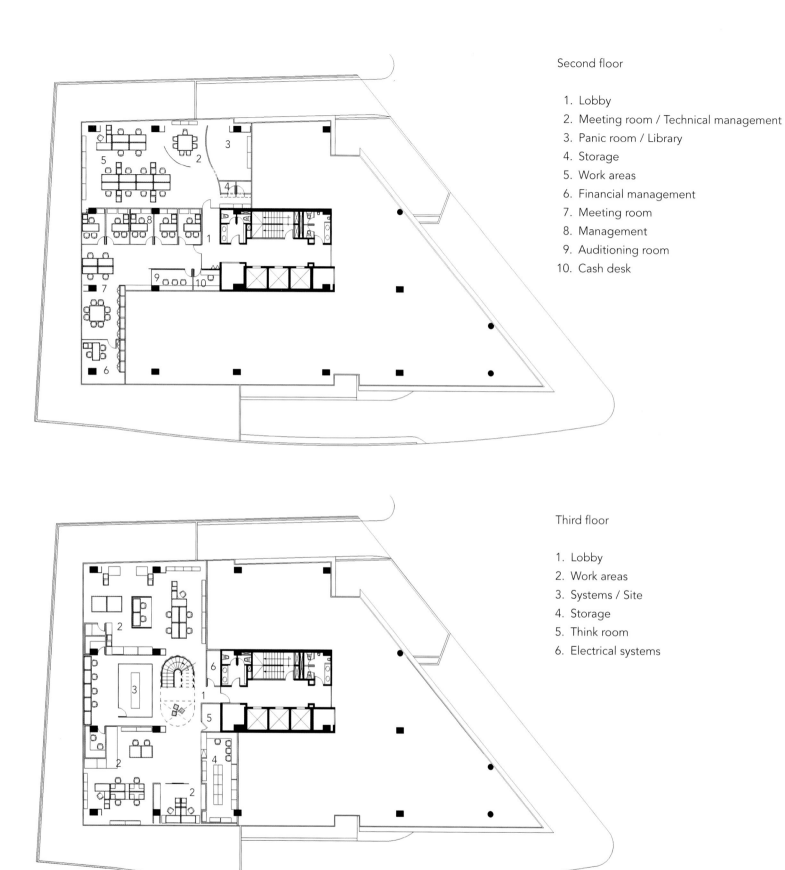

Second floor

1. Lobby
2. Meeting room / Technical management
3. Panic room / Library
4. Storage
5. Work areas
6. Financial management
7. Meeting room
8. Management
9. Auditioning room
10. Cash desk

Third floor

1. Lobby
2. Work areas
3. Systems / Site
4. Storage
5. Think room
6. Electrical systems

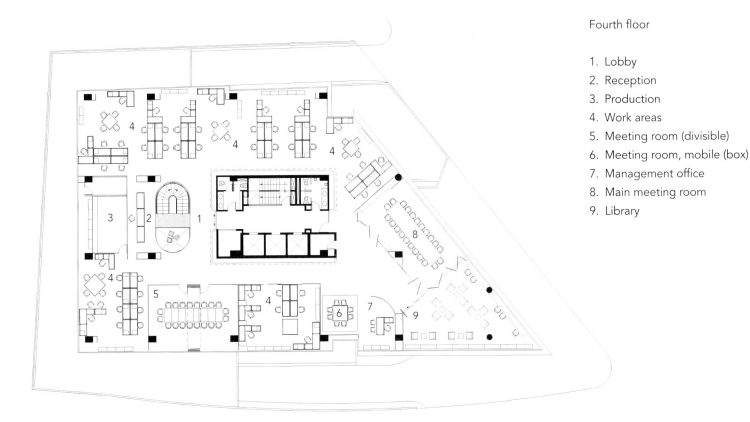

Fourth floor

1. Lobby
2. Reception
3. Production
4. Work areas
5. Meeting room (divisible)
6. Meeting room, mobile (box)
7. Management office
8. Main meeting room
9. Library

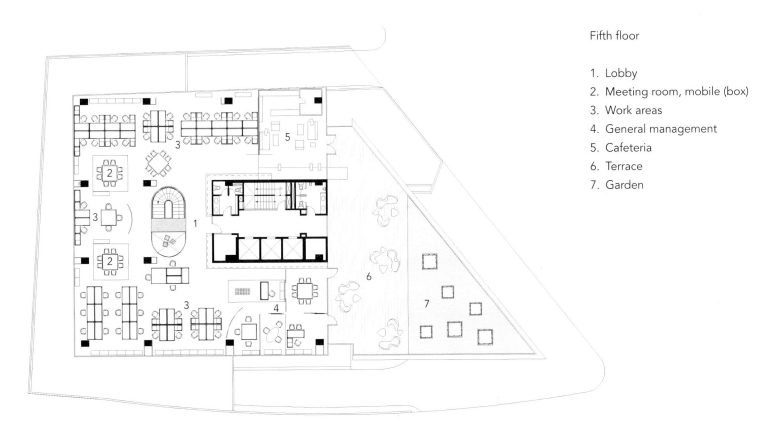

Fifth floor

1. Lobby
2. Meeting room, mobile (box)
3. Work areas
4. General management
5. Cafeteria
6. Terrace
7. Garden

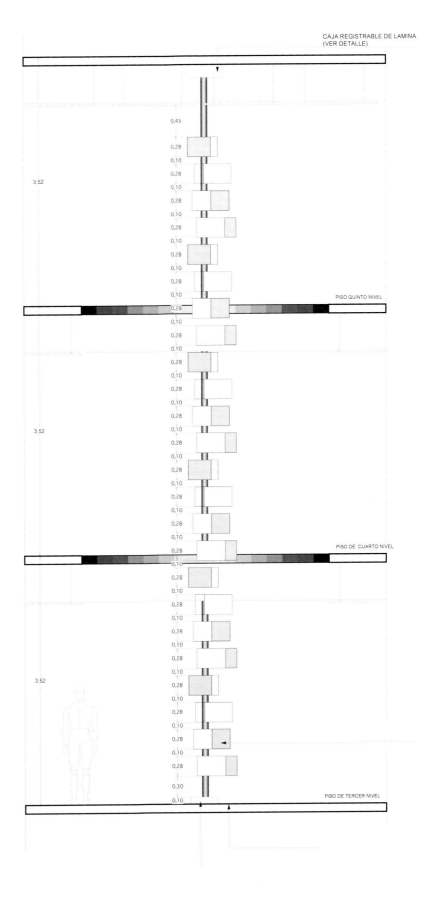

CAJA REGISTRABLE DE LAMINA
(VER DETALLE)

3.52

0,45
0,28
0,10
0,28
0,10
0,28
0,10
0,28
0,10
0,28
0,10

PISO QUINTO NIVEL

0,28
0,10

3.52

0,28
0,10
0,28
0,10
0,28
0,10
0,28
0,10
0,28
0,10
0,28
0,10

PISO DE CUARTO NIVEL

0,28
0,10

3.52

0,28
0,10
0,28
0,10
0,28
0,10
0,28
0,10
0,28
0,10
0,28
0,30
0,10

PISO DE TERCER NIVEL

The main meeting room is composed of revolving and sliding panels, and transforms into an open room integrating with the bookshelf and the hallway, and creating a large communal space.

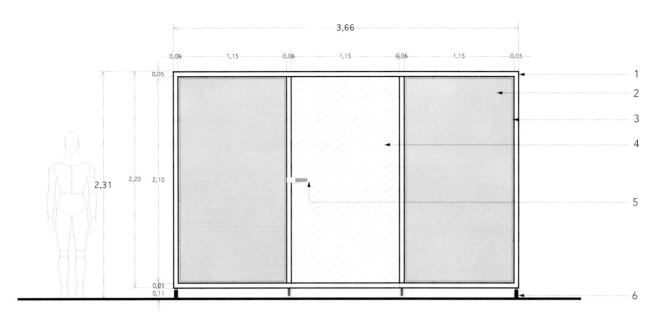

Meeting room - Box

1. Structure of 2″× 2‴ Prolamsa angle irons
2. Solid wood modules, looking like particle board
3. Aluminum angle to fix panel
4. Door of tempered glass
5. Ply sheet, front and back
6. Wheels with breaks, Cymisa catalogue

Detail of niches

1. Sheets of wood to clad the legs of the structure
2. Metal channel
3. Concrete fill and slab
4. Posts clad with SMA sheeting
5. Semitransparent acrylic siding over the entire structure
6. Interior siding of MDF with a finish of orange lacquer
7. Exterior siding of MDF finished with black blackboard-paint
8. Wood sheet niche, finished with car-paint

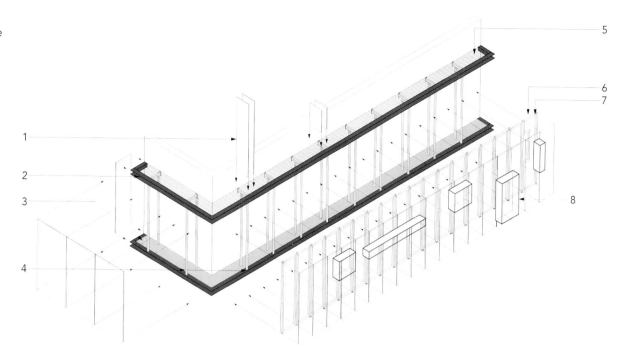

The few existing walls, composed of panels of white slate
or glass, can be easily moved.

The cafeteria has a large communal sofa that invites communication, and continues outside forming part of the terrace.

Uras + Dilekci Architects

SBS Showroom

Istanbul, Turkey

Photographs:
contributed by the architects

Architects:

Uras + Dilekci Architects,

Emir Uras y Durmus Dilekci

Project architect:

Sinan Paker

Client:

SBS, Niso Ipekel

The team of architects behind this project, headed by Emir Uras and Durmus Dilekci, are known for their highly creative designs, which draw on research into futuristic building systems.

SBS, an Istanbul-based shirt manufacturer, commissioned this local studio to transform their new premises, a former sweet factory, situated on the Asian side of Istanbul. The resulting space is a clear, open-plan area, of shiny white surfaces, with high ceilings and a minimalist style.

The building that houses this project is comprised of two floors. All production is carried out on the upper floor and the design team, showrooms and meeting rooms are located on the ground floor. (800 sqm or 8600 sqft)

Uras + Dilekci Architects were responsible for designing two showrooms, which are equipped with a remote conveyor system that transports the shirts directly to the meeting tables, where they hang on display. The main meeting table is located on a cocoon-shaped platform, which wraps around to create an intimate space where the shirts are presented and prices are discussed. Again, everything found in this area has been painted white to direct the emphasis and focus towards the articles of clothing on display. The bizarrely shaped lights, which hang from the ceiling here, are also highly effective in fulfilling this role.

The designers work on ping-pong tables that fold up, when needed, to reduce the space they occupy, and which have been fitted with wheels allowing them to be easily moved. Above these a system of fluorescent strip lighting offers ample illumination to these unique and playful work surfaces. The architects also came up with the design for a storage unit, which was intended to be used by the designers, and serves as a container for materials and accessories.

All the spaces are divided, separated and insulated by custom-made remote PVC doors.

There is an espresso bar, which wraps around one of the columns standing in the main space, offering respite to those working in the building, and also acting as a waiting area for potential clients and visitors. The seating for this area is in the form of small white blocks, which serve as stools where people can rest.

The reception area juts out from a single-step platform, which welcomes the clients into this open and fluid space.

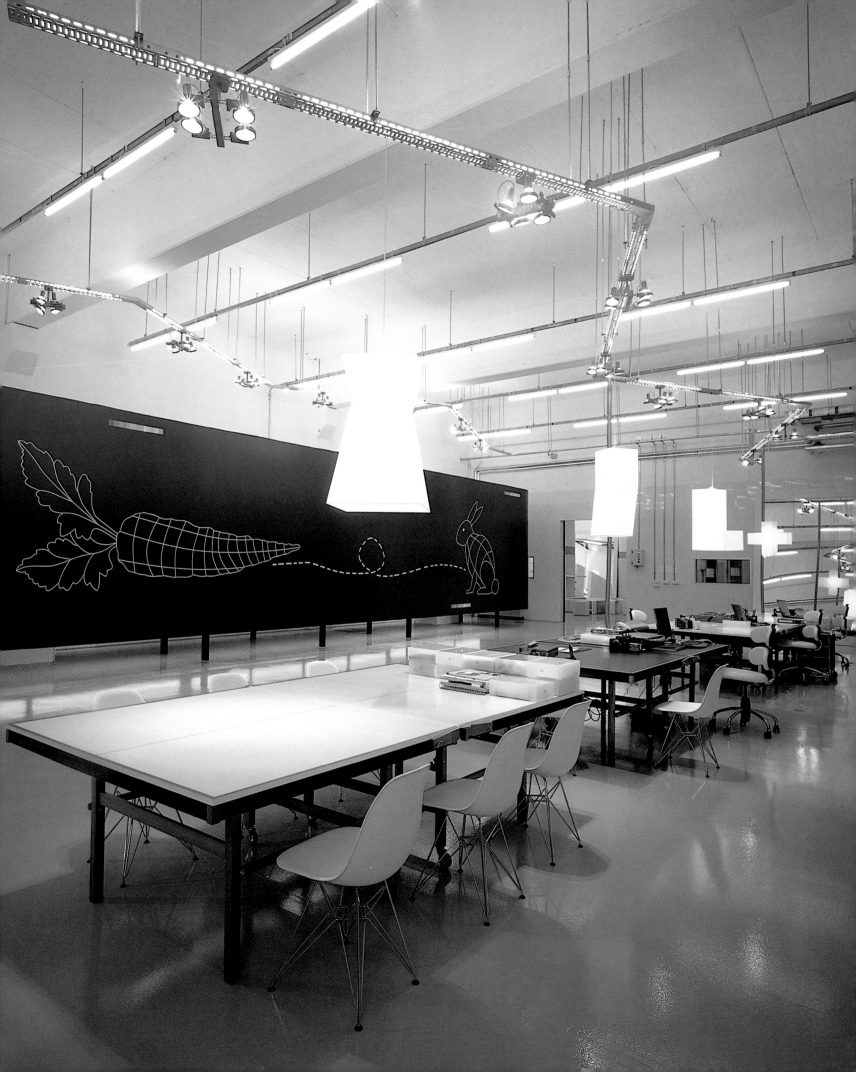

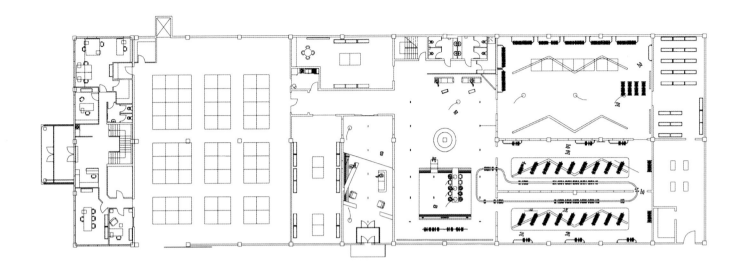

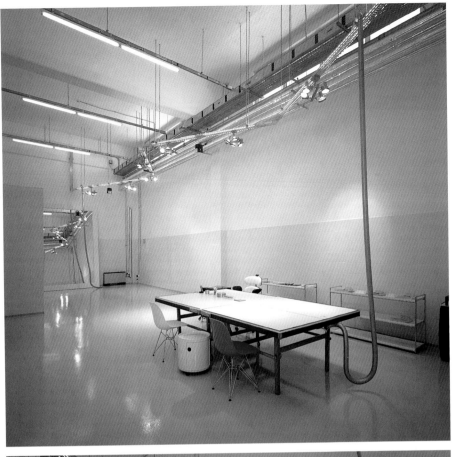

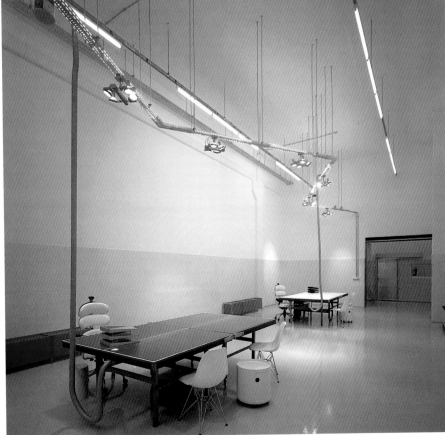

Carlos Valls

Producer of Advertising Spots

Barcelona, Spain

Photographs:
Enric Duch

This work space, belonging to an advertising producer, occupies an old industrial building, situated in the interior courtyard of the well-known "Eixample" district in Barcelona, formed from the typical octagonal blocks and with a central courtyard that defines Ildefons Cerdà's urban plan. The 23 ft high building, preserves the cast-iron pillars and the original truss beams, made from compound metal girders and riveted joins.

The project had to adhere to a specific program, with both performance spaces and work spaces. The concept used to develop the interior began with two closed, opaque boxes and a mezzanine that stretches right across the back of the space.

This volumetric arrangement creates a significant access point, that measures the entire height of the building, and areas for individual offices in the mezzanine, with smaller dimensions. The two boxes, of pure appearance, are used respectively for management offices, defined by anodized aluminum, and a storage space, constructed with black unpolished iron panels.

One important aspect of all the communal, domestic and interstitial spaces was the light. Skylights have been built into the roof at strategic points, providing natural light throughout the building; for the communal spaces, the offices and the director's office, and creating particular experiences at each point of the project.

The ground floor space has wide circulation areas with no obstacles to break up the fluidity. The interior is sober and elegant thanks to the combination of the hard concrete and stainless steel of the floors and walls on the first floor and the warmth of the wood on the stairs, the minimalist lines and mezzanine floor. A double-height wall painted orange breaks with the natural tones of the dominant materials, and adds a carefree flavor, capable of capturing all the light from the skylights and of having a life of its own, like a curtain in the background onto which the large slabs of concrete and the first flight of stairs are projected.

This is a bare, versatile space, full of character and executed using a minimal palette of materials.

Architect:
Carlos Valls
Structural engineer:
Pau Benach
Mechanical engineer:
Jordi Fernández, (Intemax)
Constructor:
Salvador Codinacs (Kunter-Lak sl)
Total surface:
838 sqm (9016 sqft)

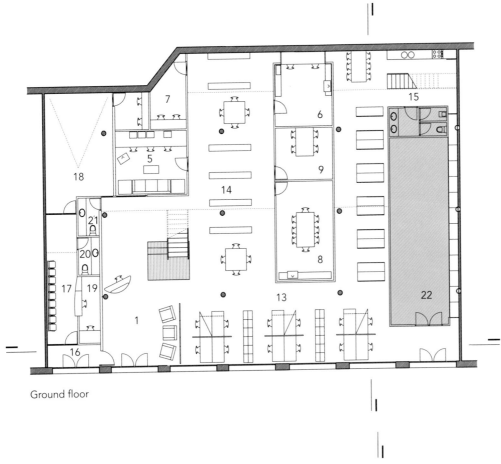

1. Reception
2. Management
3. Accounting
4. Coordination
5. Digital editing
6. BTC
7. Cast editing
8. Large hall
9. Little hall
10. Producer
11. Production managers
12. Directors
13. Production
14. Common production
15. Toilets
16. Vestibule
17. Waiting room
18. Set
19. Office
20. Dressing room
21. Bathroom
22. Stage prop storage room
23. Back storage room

Ground floor

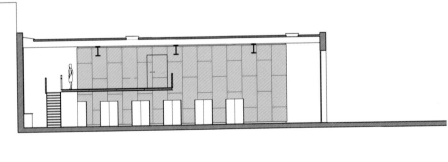

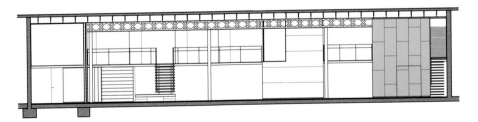

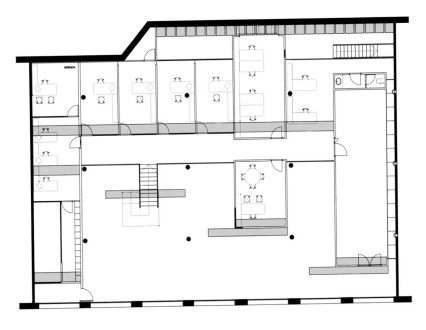

HASSELL

Investa Property Group

Sydney, Australia

Photographs:
Tyrone Branigan

Investa Property Group's new workplace occupies two levels (total area approximately 2.880 sqm,30.990 sqft) in the prestigious Norman Foster skyscraper 'Deutsche Bank Place' at 126 Phillip Street in Sydney, a building which is itself part of this successful young company's portfolio. The fitout by architects and designers Hassell was the first Green Star Office Interior to achieve 5 stars in Sydney, based on Australia's Green Building Council's standards. One of the world's top real estate groups in terms of sustainability performance it was essential that their own workplace should reflect these core values.

This flagship development has consolidated Investa's various offices and some 200 employees into one space. The design optimises space within the workplace, allowing efficiency and flexibility of use. Investa's aim was to provide a showcase of their aspirations for a friendly, effective, interactive and sustainable office. The clarity and transparency enable visitors to 'experience' the Investa work environment. Furthermore being on the two low-rise floors in the new tower means anyone in the high speed glazed lifts will view their offices before those of any other company. The clear circulation routes to public activities within the office, avoiding traffic through quiet work zones, are quite evident.

The workspace itself is generous, accommodating the varied needs of the different business groups, while maintaining a consistent appearance. Utility and storage points are evenly distributed and in close proximity to the teams, while there are a variety of flexible work settings including formal meeting rooms, breakout spaces and casual stop points. Despite the office's position on the lower floors, light comes from the spectacular atrium, a key feature of the Foster building.

In keeping with the client's environmentally aware principles the designers needed to consider the most appropriate materials and products. In fact the green Vitra screen and graphic motifs were originally unrelated to the 'green' sustainable approach although in the end they served a double purpose. The idea actually evolved from one of the key early design concepts: to shift focus internally rather than externally and create a natural 'outdoor' environment indoors as an extension of the atrium, in response to the site and surrounding environment. Together with the other 'natural' finishes like the timber panelling and the recycled rubber flooring, this green screening enhances the sense of a 'natural' environment indoors, rather than being a literal reference to a sustainable design approach. The graphic film motifs evolved from the Vitra screens as a further extension of this theme.

There is no doubt that Hassell's contribution to this project has effectively supported the company's corporate objectives and enhanced effective operations for all aspects of the business.

Interior Designers:
HASSELL
Project team:
Josephine Cole, Caroline Diesner, Neille Hepworth, Ken Maher, Meredith Proctor, Tom Rogers, Marisa Sidoti, Mark Talbot, Dana Tomic
Design and Construction Manager:
Bovis Lend Lease
Mechanical Electrical & Lighting Engineers:
Norman Disney & Young
Fire Engineer:
Warren Smith & Partners
Hydraulic Engineers:
LHO Group
Fire Compliance:
Stephen Grubits & Associates
AV Consultant:
Oriel / Pivod
BCA Certification:
McKenzie Group
Storage Consultant:
Proactive Information Solutions
Quantity Surveyor:
Davis Langdon
Acoustic Consultant:
Acoustic Logic Consultancy
ESD Consultant:
Kirsty Mate
Client:
Investa Property Group

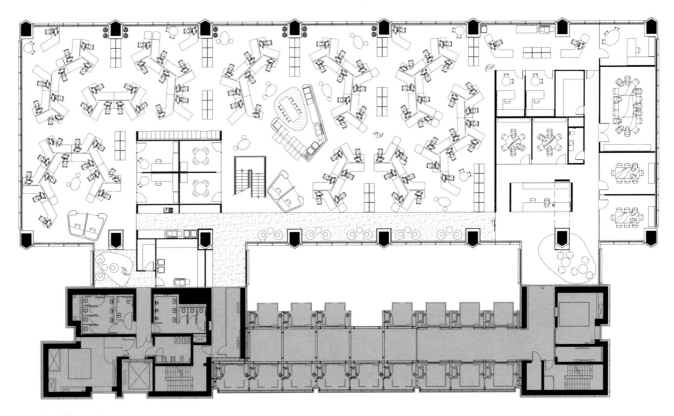

Sixth floor plan

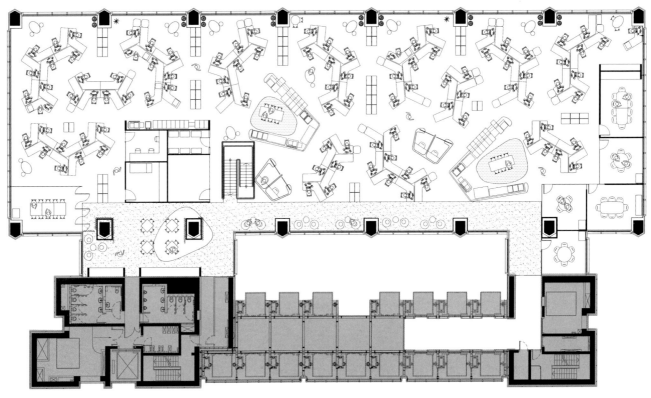

Seventh floor plan

For the all-important 120 degree workstations Abak Environments by Herman Miller was selected for its high quality and flexibility as a modular system. The random style layout allows freedom of movement and encourages collaboration and teamwork through the varied circulation paths. The workstation materials were also selected with sustainability in mind: EO board substrates on desktops, Woven Image 'Echopanel' screens (recyclable textiles made from partially recycled material), and powder coated joinery where possible to reduce use of adhesives/formaldehydes.

In keeping with the client's environmentally aware principles the designers needed to consider the most appropriate materials and products. Together with the other 'natural' finishes like the timber panelling and the recycled rubber flooring, the green screening enhances the sense of a 'natural' environment indoors, rather than being a literal reference to a sustainable design approach. The graphic film motifs evolved from the Vitra screens as a further extension of this theme.

The workspace is generous accommodating the varied needs of the different business groups, while maintaining a consistent appearance. Utility and storage points are evenly distributed and in close proximity to the teams, while there are a variety of flexible work settings including formal meeting rooms, breakout spaces and casual stop points.

Jump Studios

Red Bull HQ

London, UK

Photographs:
Gareth Gardner

Encouraging interaction between employees while communicating the company's brand values and identity were the dual aims of the design of Red Bull's new 1860 sqm (20 000 sqft) headquarters, projected by London-based, multidisciplinary architecture and design studio, Jump Studios. The resulting £2m offices stimulate employees and visitors alike, through a stunning interior, which generates adrenalin and adds a sense of dynamic excitement; emotions associated with the Red Bull brand and its various activities.

The brief was to amalgamate two separate offices into one central headquarters building, located in London's Soho district. The new offices occupy the top three floors of an existing 19th century building, and include a recent roof-level extension in the form of a glass "box" surrounded by an exterior terrace, providing spectacular views of the West End.

This, according to Jump Studios' director himself, Simon Jordan, represents an ideal starting point for both employees and visitors alike, as a way for them to experience the building. They arrive by lift into the top-floor public reception and social zone, before descending through the building. This sense of descent is enhanced by voids punched through the building's fabric, providing vertiginous views. A three-story video wall occupies one void, while another includes a dramatic circulation system, consisting of a floating staircase and even a slide, aimed at encouraging free movement through the spaces.

The design team has succeeded in creating an open, efficient, dynamic and connected workspace. The top floor acts as a social hub, containing the main reception, bar, café, both informal and formal meeting areas, plus the main boardroom. They are all in continual use throughout the day, both for company activities and to encourage interaction. These top floor features are "stitched" together by a continuous, snaking carbon-fiber element, which runs from the exterior terrace (providing a wing canopy) through the building, encapsulating the main boardroom, forming the reception area, before disappearing through a void to form the enclosure for the slide and support for the staircase. It terminates on the lower floor as a platform, creating an informal meeting area. The feature evokes the trace patterns left by skaters, snowboarders, stunt planes, race cars and bikes, symbolizing Red Bull's commitment to placing adrenalin sport at the heart of its business.

Architects:
Jump Studios
Project team:
Shaun Fernandes,
Simon Jordan, Laszlo Fecske,
Go Sugimoto
Structural engineer:
Price & Meyers
Mechanical and Electrical engineers:
Faber Maunsell
General contractor:
IBEX Interiors
Furniture dealer:
twentytwentyone
Client:
Red Bull UK Ltd
Total floor area:
1860 sqm (20 000 sqft)
Total cost:
2 000 000 £

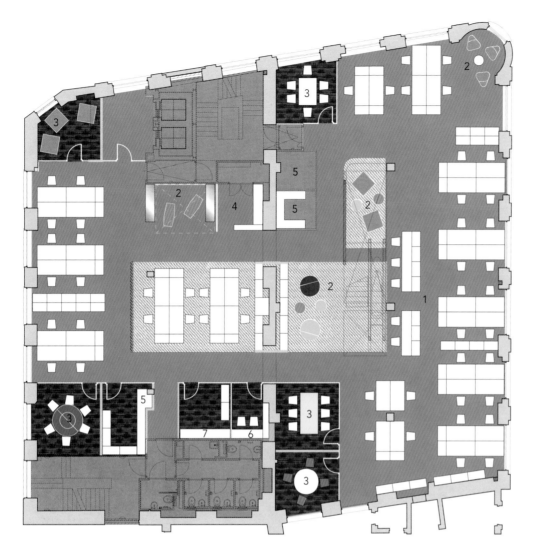

First floor

1. Hot desks
2. Break-out
3. Meeting room
4. Teapoint
5. Storage
6. Editing room
7. Administration

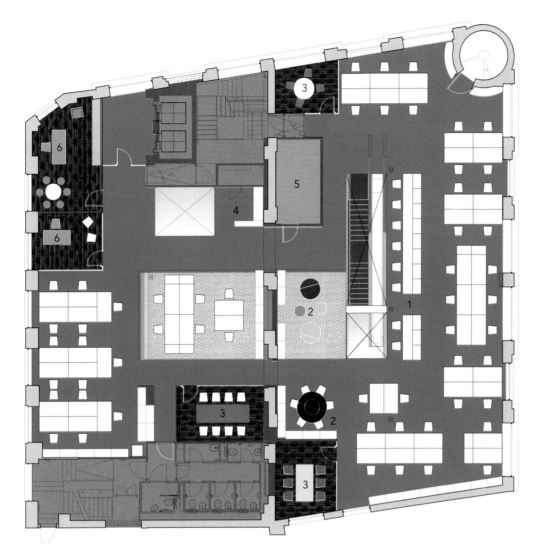

Second floor

1. Hot desks
2. Break-out
3. Meeting room
4. Teapoint
5. Comms room
6. Offices

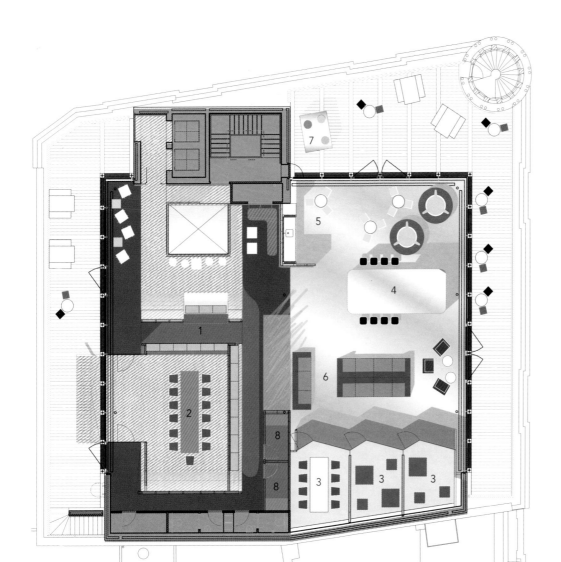

Third floor

1. Reception
2. Board room
3. Meeting room
4. Bar
5. Kitchen
6. Lounge
7. Smokers hut
8. Changing room

Delugan Meissl Associated Architects

Global Headquarters Sandoz

Vienna, Austria

Photographs:
Rupert Steiner

The point of departure is the close relation between the surroundings, the spatial fabric and the proper functioning processes within a system. For Novartis the spatial concept is based on a number of fundamental factors that generate specific spatial fabrics:
The potential of each individual to identify with his/her spatial surroundings.
The potential to transform the context in which he/she operates, in this case the company philosophy, into expression in spatial terms. Networked, creative, innovative thinking that is reflected in the spatial context and can be experienced by means of flowing, transparent, unobstructed spatial configurations. Regarding the existing structure, the initially neutral space is the point of departure for a spatial concept based on the given situation, yet unfolding its own architectural identity.
NovaMobile, the flexible shelf system developed especially for Novartis, forms the basis of the interior design of the office spaces:
The shelf system's basic function is separation of access ways and office spaces, but it also forms zones of differing density and transparency – depending on the requirements and communication values of each given place. The combination of different module types, plus variable assembly possibilities permit the parallel formulation of closed-off areas, semitransparent zones, and areas of absolute transparency in different communication and work spaces. All in one, NovaMobile is a space-defining element and visual guideline.
The graphic linearity of the module system, as opposed to the organic patterned screen lit from behind, makes the hallway into an energy-charged place whose impact emphasizes the vastness of the spatial impression and goes beyond the functional. In the lobby, the linear module system takes on the distinct contours of an object – the reception desk – allowing a transition from the hallway's tight clarity to an open gesture of arrival.

Architecture:
Delugan Meissl Associated Architects
Project team:
Martin Josst
Christopher Schweiger
Interior construction:
Novartis Company / IZD Tower
Project management:
Gobiet & Partner
Structural consultant:
Werkraum Wien
Realization:
bsw19
Acoustics:
David Haigner
Carpentry works:
Barth / List
Graphics:
section d
Client:
BC Biochemie Pharma GmbH
Start of construction:
2002
Completion:
2003
Building costs:
1 870 500 €
Floor area:
2900 sqm (31 204 sqft)
Gross surface area:
3600 sqm (38 730 sqft)

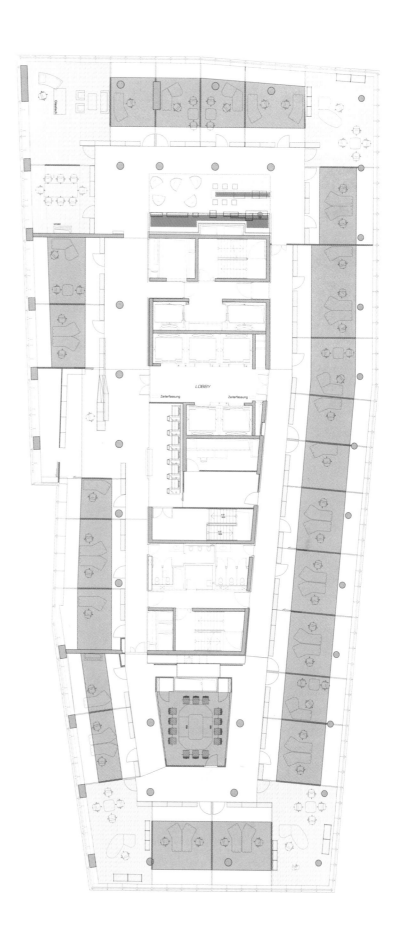

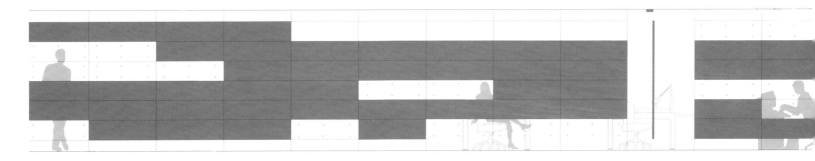

In the lounge the principle of modules attached to the glass walls changes: a kitchen unit, boxes, and shelves pierce a floor-to-ceiling-high glass box filled with plants. In front of this is a counter consisting of various boxes with kitchen gear and another glass box with plants. Greenery used as architectural units creates an atmosphere of freshness, relaxation, and inspiration.

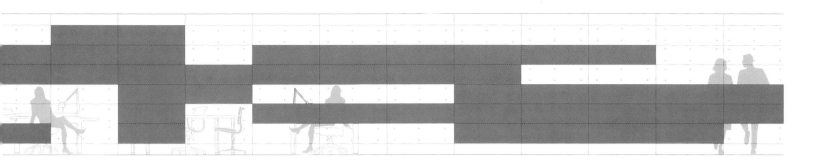

The shelf system can be accessed from the office as well as from the hallway. The components consist of shelves, open and closed boxes, and greenery units. These are mounted on the walls of the floor-to-ceiling glass elements; their arrangement and number is determined by their specific use. The rear surfaces of these modules produce a pattern visible from the hallway.

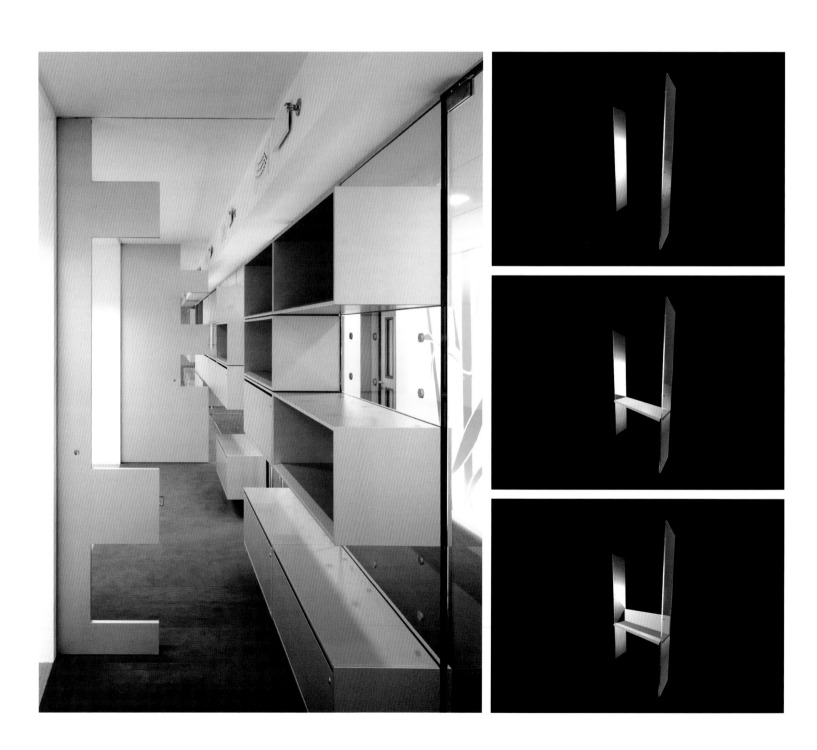

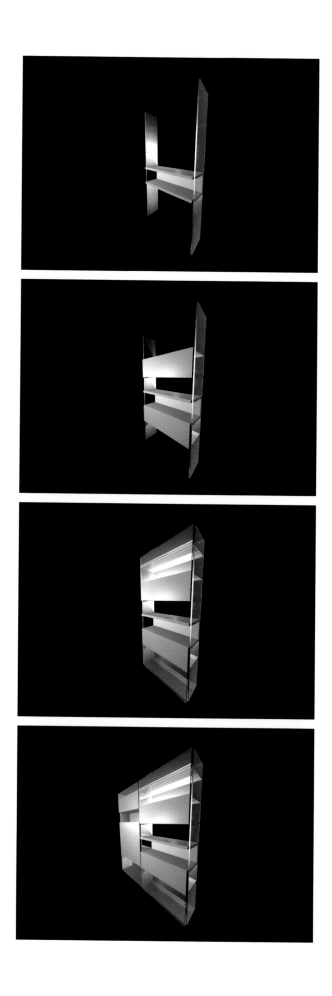
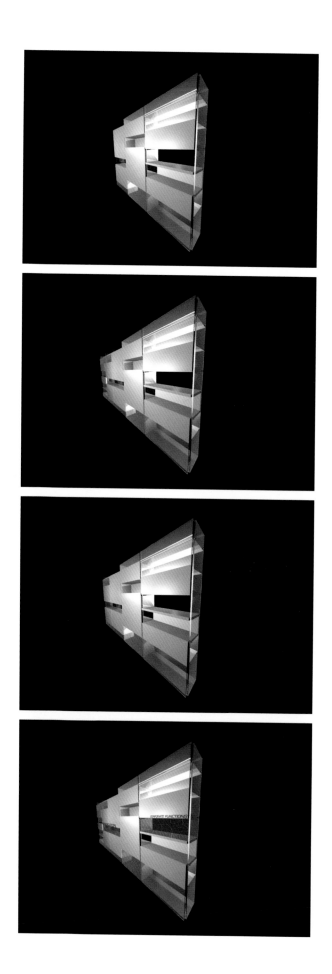

What is inherent in the spatial fabric is that it is composed of very different places and situations, which come together and allow complex and manifold interactions to occur. Space, as a place of meeting has the potential for promoting communication as an essential component of that place. Great importance, therefore, has been placed on the communication areas, the reception desk, lounge, and kitchen.

Artistic Image / Artemis Creative

Atlanta, Georgia, USA

Photographs:
Lance Davies

Artistic Image and Artemis Creative headquartered in Atlanta, Georgia, serve high profile clients such as the NFL, Coca Cola, The Golf Channel, Pepsi, and Ford Motor corp. As both design studios work with clients that may be in direct competition with one another, it was a primary goal to maintain separate identities for each, while at the same time allowing them to collaborate and use the same resources. The ability to design a space that embodied the spirit of one company's particular brand was not an avenue the design could pursue. Rather, the focus aimed towards designing a space that embodied and defined what it means to be "creative". The design solution employed was the insertion of an above ground "tunnel to transport employees and visitors into the world of creativity and protect two businesses from each other"

Structured with plywood ribs and sheathed in translucent plastics, the tunnel allows for discrete passage from the main entry to one group's studio space on the lower level. The tunnel is lit from within, thereby also serving as a translucent stage that illuminates and projects the interior activity to the studios beyond. The bent plastic distorts the light, creating unique and ever-changing reflections within the space. A white epoxy coating on the concrete floors helps to reflect and bounce light into the inner areas of the space.

The other studio, located on a central mezzanine, is accessed by a "hidden" stairway located behind the feature wall that supports the tunnel. The mezzanine, itself, intended to blend with the lightness and loftiness of the upper clerestory, uses a minimalist approach with cable rail guards for continual light to reach the mezzanine from all possible levels and angles. From high above, the translucent tunnel's fifth elevation is revealed, which reflects light inboard into the space. This group is also given the ability to interact with the existing structural steel trusses, creating a space that is totally connected and immersed within the building itself, and reminds the group of the building's historic importance and presence.

Architects:
ai3
www.ai3online.com
Client:
Artistic Image
Completion:
June 2006
Surface:
370 sqm (4000 sqft)

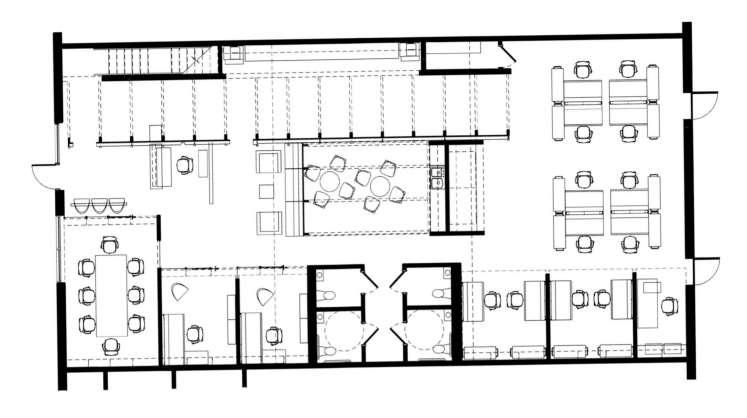

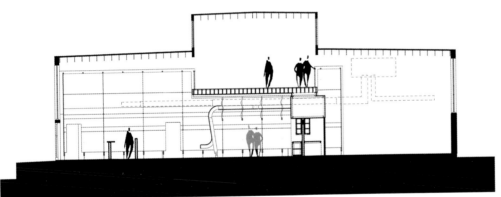

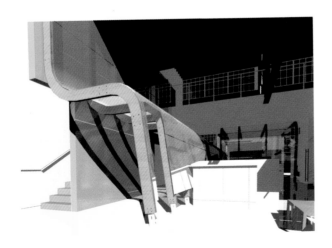

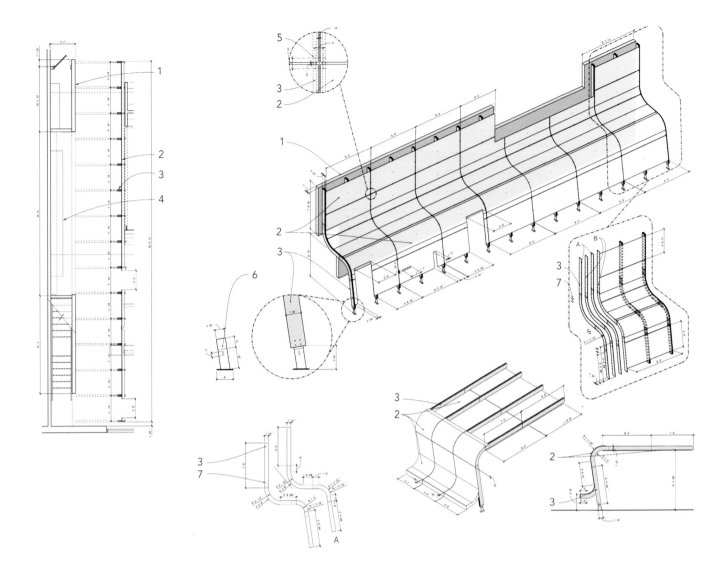

1. Gypsum board wall assembly
2. Traslucent acrylic panels
3. 4 layers 3/4″ plywood
4. Plastic laminate cabinet and shelving
5. Counter sunk metal fastner
6. 1/4″ steel plate
7. 1/2″ dowels

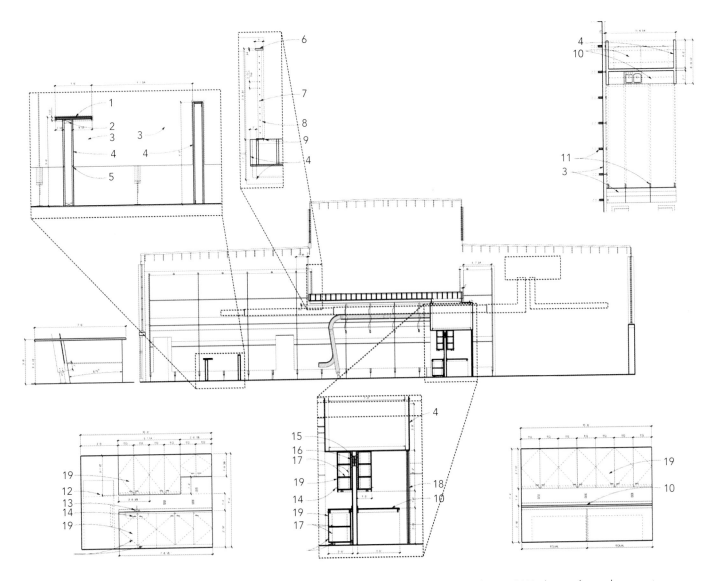

1. Solid surface counter on 3/4″ substrate
2. Wood blocking
3. Translucent acrylic panels
4. Gypsum wallboard
5. 1/2″ × 1/2″ molded reveal
6. Wood cap
7. 1/8″ diameter 316 steel cable
8. 2 × 2″ aluminium guardrail post
9. 5″ square base plate fastened to wood deck with stainless steel lag bots
10. 3/4″ substrate layout counter with plastic laminate finish on exposed surfaces

11. 4 layers 3/4″ plywood panel support
12. Refrigerator
13. Sink
14. Cabinet door pull
15. 2″ × 10″ fire retardant wood blocking
16. Wood cleat mounting
17. White melamine adjustable shelf
18. Painted solid core wood sliding doors on embedded tracks
19. 3/4″ substrate door with plastic laminate finish on exposed surfaces

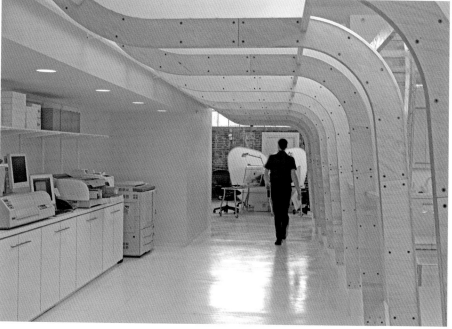